THE WAY OF THE ORPHAN STONE

AUTHOR AND ORPHAN
DON MANNERBERG, M.D.

EDITOR AND MENTOR
JERRY CASEBOLT, D.C.

Way of the Orphan Stone

Inquiries should be addressed to

Archaic Ideas
502 W. 7th Street, #102
Austin, Texas 78701

FIRST EDITION

ISBN 978-0-615-28502-3

Cover image: Bollingen Stone

Cover design by Rebecca Byrd Bretz

Page design by Terry Sherrell

Printed in the United States of America
at Morgan Printing in Austin, Texas

DEDICATION

To the orphan in each of us,
Creative soul standing alone.
Because of its uniqueness,
Paradoxical obliqueness
By name is a treasured stone.

To the divine genius within us
Golden Chalice standing alone

Embracing its dark mass

In each candescent pass

I dedicate this book to the Stone

CONTENTS

CHARTING THE FRAY
WITHOUT A KINGDOM
WALKING THE WAY
TO SOPHIA'S WISDOM

LEVEL THREE
WALKING THE WAY
69

LEVEL ONE

CHARTING THE FRAY

"Now, we have no symbolic life, and we are all badly in need of a symbolic life. Only the symbolic life can express the needs of the soul- the daily need of the soul, mind you! And because people have no such thing, they can never step out of the mill- this awful, grinding banal life in which they are "nothing but.." Life is too rational (logical), there is no symbolic existence in which I am something else, in which I am fulfilling my role, my role as one of the actors in a divine drama."

— Carl Jung, *Collected Works*, Vol. 18, par. 627–28

CHAPTER 1

LOGOS AND MYTHOS

A modern slang definition of myth is that it has no basis in fact. When one becomes aware of mythology's truth, life itself takes on a different presence. Suddenly mythology becomes an archetypal pattern that you can identify in your own life. Does your process of thinking derive meaning for experience from Fact or is it based on Myth? Dr. Mannerberg's search for that meaning of the Stone has historical foundations, logos, and mythological connections, mythos.

What about "fact" and "truth"? A fact has historical data supporting its authenticity. A truth is something that works for years. There are two separate events taking place in the mind. Both are necessary for living. Both are necessary for making decisions. Both are necessary for making sense out of experience. Both are necessary for making sense out of life's challenges. One is not better or worse than the other; that would be like comparing apples and motorcycles. They are two different processes in the mind. One is rational. One is irrational. Psychologists separate the features of the mind into two categories; rational and irrational during analysis.

To consider these paradoxes about truth, fact, myth and history, you have to examine both psychology, and mythology. Two important paradoxical words came to your attention; Mythos, and Logos and these are at the heart of understanding the paradox inherent in life, especially in the way we suffer.

Mythos literally means to close the eyes or close the mouth, while Logos means to wrap words around something or the art of discourse; being discursive. That's what I'm doing right now; being discursive. It often gets me in trouble because whatever anyone wraps words around automatically becomes arguable because of the strong emotions that people have concerning their own truth. That's Logos in a nutshell. When we keep the feelings about our experience to ourselves as a mystery, we are not subject to argument. That's Mythos.

Plato taught that Mythos keeps running into Logos and that explains why discussions about the meaning of events tend to end up in disagreement, while our experience of the mystery usually ends up with being filled with a silent awe where explanation is fruitless.

You probably never told anyone how you felt about certain mystical experiences because there really aren't any literal words to describe it. So, it wouldn't be appropriate to tell anyone how you really felt about it. Those feelings of awe are inexplicable. That's Mythos. If you talk about it you subject yourself to criticism and you lose the power and awe of it to your own unconscious mind.

On the other hand we want to feel secure in our beliefs and connections to the past. That's what Logos brings us. If you realize this, you will know the two sides of the riddles inherent in life's encounters with experience. Look closely at the riddle in question; neither mythos nor logos; neither history nor secret knowledge.

Why and how can you apply these distinctions to Dr. Mannerberg's treatise on suffering? There is a tremendous opportunity for an application in healthcare. Consider the word disease. When you become aware that dis-ease is a condition away from ease, your awareness immediately sheds a different light upon how you perceive your experience with sickness. Dis-ease simply becomes the experience of your body in conflict; a period of inner struggle reflected from the world of mythos to the world of logos. We call illness pathology; wrapping words around pathos: suffering.

The words "symptom," to bring together, and "symbol," to throw together, are essentially the same. We can say that our symptoms are symbolic of our disease or conflicts between the conscious and unconscious. If you realize this, you will have a much better chance of understanding something of the process of suffering in life and those life-long processes during which we suffer, reflect, introspect and grow. In this way we achieve the goal of becoming conscious. Symbols and metaphors help you understand a universal connection to both the internal and external processes of life itself without the total use of words to give value to your experience. A symbol is a physical representative of a spiritual idea, whereas a symptom is a physical manifestation of an idea arising out of the unconscious.

Within the context of life there are many levels of understanding. These perspectives of Logos and Mythos, History and Myth, symptom and symbol, are but three of these levels. The quest for consciousness is about experiencing the mysteries of life and death. Life is a journey; a search for meaning; for the treasure; for the gold in the muck of suffering.

Regardless of whether you have a tendency to be a history buff or whether you have a bit of a mystical bent ask yourself, "How's my way of interpreting reality working for me? Study the history of mythology and you will experience the feelings of awe shared with millions that you are a participant in an ancient process of alchemy; experiencing the great archetypal mystery. That way you can experience the light of knowledge, the light by experience, or hopefully both. In this context light is the metaphor for making conscious that which is unconscious. If the study of mythology resonates with you, it will enhance your soul's search for meaning.

Dr. Mannerberg's experience and wisdom are his most valued gift to us all. He exemplifies the true meaning of Doctor: "Teacher." This is the good doctor's Magnum Opus; a gift of the Ritual Elder.

Jerry Casebolt, D.C.

CHAPTER 2

BOLLINGEN STONE

Introduction

An orphan who became a physician in a lifelong quest for healing has, at this late stage of life, received the message of The Stone that introduced me to a state of being which gave meaning to the challenges of an atypical life. Journaling the life experiences crossing my path has deepened the appreciation and confirmed the creative value of The Stone.

The mythos found in Hermetic wisdom is presented to us by the Works of Carl Jung. Jung claimed the inscription on his orphan stone at Bollingen represented "his inner most thoughts which remain incomprehensible to others." I found that Jung's wisdom has given me a comprehensible way by which to identify and explore my own struggles with understanding life, and my role in a divine drama.

The contents of this book present the Way of the Stone as a process and metaphor whereby adversity is honored for its transformative value. It is an archetypal creative process activated during trying experiences of my life which tested my endurance and faith. There are times when an individual becomes an Orphan, feels abandoned or victimized by major loss for which there seems to be no traditionally accepted resolution or refuge. It is this essential drama that motivates all our struggles be they personal or universal.

The Stone displayed on the front cover of this book, the Bollingen stone, was sculpted by Carl Jung during 1950. The story of how the stone came to Jung is curious. Stones for added construction to the Tower at Bollingen were delivered. The cornerstone was discovered to be a misfit. When the mason rejected it Jung responded, "No, that is my stone, I must have it." He then recalled a phrase from alchemy:

Here the mean uncomely stone
'Tis very cheap in price
The more despised by fools
The more loved by the wise.

The Stone is an appropriate metaphor for the metamorphism of the soul and I have chosen it as a proper symbol for my own understanding of suffering.

Jung's Inscription

Jung said, "In remembrance of my seventy-fifth birthday I had to make a confession in stone, a representative in stone of my most inner most thoughts. On the third surface of the stone, I let the stone itself speak in a Latin inscription. The sayings are more or less from alchemy. It is a manifestation of the occupant, but which remains incomprehensible to others. It gave me a feeling of being reborn in stone."[1]

The translation of these sayings from Latin is interpreted as follows. It resonates with my own sense of value as a metaphor for the projection of my own persona so that I have a sense of it.

I AM AN ORPHAN ALONE; NEVERTHELESS I AM FOUND EVERYWHERE. I AM ONE, BUT OPPOSED TO MYSELF. I AM YOUTH AND OLD MAN AT ONE AND THE SAME TIME. I HAVE KNOWN NEITHER FATHER NOR MOTHER, BECAUSE I HAVE TO BE FETCHED OUT OF THE DEEP LIKE A FISH OR FALL LIKE A WHITE STONE FROM THE HEAVEN. IN WOODS AND MOUNTAINS I ROAM, BUT I AM HIDDEN IN THE INNER MOST SOUL OF MEN. I AM MORTAL FOR EVERYONE, YET I AM NOT TOUCHED BY THE CYCLE OF EONS.[2]

Understanding the archetypal message Jung has given to us with this inscription is dependent on the capacity for mythos, symbolic cognition, clearly defined by Jerry Casebolt with his introduction. The stone message seems incomprehensible, and may seem foolish to a mind completely attached to logos whereby fiction and nonfiction are tightly bound in neat packages. Art and poetry are primary expressions of unresolved suffering.

It comprises a "rock solid" compartmentalized interpretation of reality whose response to suffering must manifest a savior to palliate or take it away. Therefore writing a book, Way of the Orphan Stone, could well be equated to expressing a feeling of frustration when attempting to converse in a foreign language to the audience. It is wrapping words around mythos.

The Challenge

A Charles Schulz *Peanuts* cartoon gave me a sense of this frustration. Linus while talking to Lucy, "why should I get rid of my blanket, why? Give me a good reason. If you can give me a good reason why, I will get rid of it."

Lucy, "Because it makes you look stupid, that's why. It makes you look stupid, silly, and arrogant."

Linus, "I knew you couldn't think of a good reason."

Simply said, I guess I could not think of a good reason not to address the vital issues concerning my struggles with the problem of suffering. The Way of the Orphan Stone is my blanket, my foolishness, a context for processing my personal adversity. At this time in my life I am desperately challenged by a crucial loss of my son. My astray orphan archetype does not process emotions according to the various interpretations and therapies favored by mainstream thinking.

Therefore, it seems that I am an ideological "misfit." I recognize the risk of being seen as a foolish old man rather than projecting an archetype which I address later in the book. Fortunately, in this modern era I will not be physically "stoned" to death. Instead I see myself judged as foolishly intoxicated, "stoned," for eating of the "forbidden" fruit.

I feel my journey has led me to the brink of some ancient mystery whose advocates always warn the mundane of the dangers of embarking on such a journey with such words as, "beware all who enter here". On the other hand, I have also learned that without the entrance into those secret chambers of darkness there is neither food for the soul nor hope for understanding mythos.

There is no doubt, "One only knows what one has experienced." The subsequent chapters of this manuscript will present those happenings which have communicated the meaning and value of Stone consciousness to me. The question arises: how does an interested individual "walk this walk"? Each person, when existentially challenged, by definition of the Stone invites exploration of the unique journey to the temple of archetypal mystery. Many have expressed it is a lonely journey.

My journey begins as an individual, an orphan, conscious of my isolation. It is with the understanding that the truth underlying my redemption may spell damnation for others. I enter a Way into unfamiliar territory forbidden by guardians of traditional values and moral judgments. Before accomplishing this feat it is required that I return to the basic facts of my being, irrespective of all authority or tradition. It is then that the Way of the Stone is activated, whereby the process of yoking is initiated and the orphan state united with my own creative center and the experience of redemption.

Joyful Expectations

Kyle

It is now late December of '07, the Christmas Holiday is approaching, and I am filled with delighted excitement in anticipation of my son Kyle's annual week long Christmas visit. My writing related to the Way of the Orphan Stone is put aside as I anticipate a week of revelry. I am relishing the prospect of embraces and intimate expressions of love and affection otherwise impossible through emails and phone conversations.

CHAPTER 3

ADVERSITY

As I reviewed my manuscript, supporting notes and references, an essential drama unfolded. Providence provided an event that tested the very fabric of my soul. I had not anticipated the complexity of my journey and learned that there is always a hidden life for each person that is slowly unveiled over time. It changed the whole text of my manuscript.

On the evening of Dec. 20, after an enlightening visit with a friend, I casually approached the darkness of my front porch. I was delightfully surprised because in the shadows stood two dear friends. My delight turned to puzzlement because they seemed more saddened than I expected. Though alarmed I simply say:

"Hi! It is great to see y'all."

Unlocking the door, we went inside. When comfortably seated I asked, "What are y'all up to?"

Jennifer turned to me with a quivering voice, eyes tearing and announced: "It is about Kyle".

"Is he gone"?

She responded: "Yes"!

"That is not possible," I said. I was in a state of instant shock. There is no vocabulary expressing my instant grief. I was devastated. My soul was "dismembered" and my body froze. Only the parent who faces this tragic moment could possibly "know".

My confused mind next asked, "How did it happen?"

Jennifer responded, "He died suddenly at home while alone. An autopsy will be done." The question of causality was but a fleeting thought quickly vanishing within the dark cloud of my sorrow.

19

At the age of 78, I was faced with an unimaginable and difficult irony: I should have died before Kyle. I had anticipated that my sole remaining major encounter with the beloved Trickster would be my initiation into the transpersonal dimension. Somehow my own child had interrupted the natural order of logic and sent me deeper into the irrational world of mythos.

Grief

In the back of my mind I recognized my psychological conflict. In the initial stages of bereavement I personally encountered the involuntary process of my grief. It was extremely tragic. Typical rational thinking demanded that I face the fact that Kyle was gone where all that remained were dry ashes and cherished memories.

Initially my grief drove me into a period of emotional turmoil of a father who only knows a personal loss. At the same time, I was aware of a seemingly conflicting idea that there was something providential and required my utmost effort to understand.

Psychology, religion, and philosophy have their ideological concepts for interfacing and processing the grief of my loss with methods for recovery. Those schemes work well for the majority of society but provided no escape from suffering for me. In addition, scientific medicine provides pills to palliate suffering but my own loss was beyond palliation. In contradiction to those common therapeutic modalities, the Way of the Orphan Stone has provided me with a unique attitudinal, process by which to integrate the logos of my loss with the mythos of my life long process and growth.

"Myths are clues to the spiritual potentialities of the human life, what you are capable of knowing and experiencing within. You change the definition of myth from the search for meaning to the experience of meaning. Our life experiences on the purely physical plane will have resonances within our innermost being and reality."[1]

Kyle's death tests my devotion to the Way of the Stone. It is a challenge for me to "wrap words around it" and to find reference points which facilitate the reader's understanding and to stimulate receptivity in those of you who wish to know a different way to engage grief and suffering, contradictory to the paradigm of our modern culture where one is limited to escapism and palliation of suffering. The art of logos has become the primary mode of creating everyday reality.

Nevertheless, my process of healing has begun. The mysterious Trickster has presented me with a colossal adversity. My most cherished loved one was taken from me. It is my ultimate challenge and initiates me deeper into Way of the Orphan Stone. My quest is to find fact in fiction, truth in myth, as it relates to Kyle's unique life and the fateful event of his departure from this world.

The process of the Stone is not present to palliate my suffering, but to involve me in a dynamism which manifests specific features that have values and meanings in my life. Whereby I am endowed with a wisdom manifested beyond any logical or emotional determinates which traditionally attempts to interpret the nature of life events. My errant Way opens me to the mythic function of my soul. It makes me receptive to those symbolic images underlying all experience; the mystery of archetypes, the journey of an Errant Orphan as Jung elaborated and will be addressed later in the text.

I honor my son Kyle in the spirit of the creative gamesmanship that earned him the title of Lead Level Designer in that world. I feel that each of the twelve chapters in this book represent progressive levels of awakening candescence while engaging the Way of the Stone. It is a gamesmanship that in the context of the first three levels eventually leads to the Wisdom of Sophia. At this fourth level of The Way my suffering soul transforms into a renewed state of being whereby Kyle and I, together celebrate our archetypal reunion. My subjective grief becomes united with its divine healer.

LEVEL TWO

WITHOUT A KINGDOM

"I am orphan, alone, nevertheless I am one, but opposed to myself. I have known neither father nor mother. In woods and mountains I roam, but I am hidden in the innermost soul of man. I am mortal for everyone, yet I am untouched by the cycle of eons."

— Jung, Carl, The Orphan Stone Inscription.

"The provisional life denotes an attitude that is innocent of the responsibility towards the circumstantial facts of reality as though these facts are being provided for, either by the parents, or the state, or at least providence. . . it is a state of childish irresponsibility and dependence."

— Baynes, H.C., The Provisional Life.

CHAPTER 4

THE ERRANT ORPHAN

*P*eanuts cartoonist Charles Schulz offers a unique insight into Stone wisdom. While Lucy is standing with Linus, she picks up a pebble and says to him, "Here is a nice pebble. Take it home with you and observe it. The fascinating thing about pebbles is their growth. For some grow up to be stones while others grow up to be rocks. You shall hope of course that it grows up to be a rock. For a pebble that grows up to be a stone is like a youth that has gone astray."

Lucy leaves and Linus standing alone declares, "I have so much to learn."

Rocks and Stones

In this cartoon, Charles Schulz illustrates an opportunity to differentiate between the meanings that seem logical and a lesson implied by symbolic recognition. He provides me, his adamant admirer, with another priceless source of fundamental wisdom. The issue of the Stone gone astray is crucial enough to write a whole book about it. The "all knowing" Lucy (who else), in Schulz's cast of charming characters, is the ideal banner bearer for cultural dogma, a proponent of allegory and vocal advocate espousing the culturally favored logos ideals identified with The Rock. While at same time, she devalues the symbolism of the Stone; the one who has "Gone Astray," the errant Orphan "Without a Kingdom."

In contrast the Rock symbolizes logos and the stability and firmness of rational thought. The Rock effectively serves the consciousness of the collective mind and human sense of reality concerning life's disturbing challenges. It is the accumulation of knowledge in contrast to understanding based on individual experience. That which is not susceptible to a statistical approach is the despised stone rejected by the builders of our modern paradigm.

The Way of the Stone redeems suffering by yoking both ways of thinking. In other words, it is engaging one way while not losing awareness of the other. One is then faced with evaluating the sick person as a unique individual in addition to the use of statistical tools provided by science. The art of vocabulary becomes the primary mode of creating logos reality.

You see this in our science bound culture which demands that the capacity to respond logically and the ability to communicate factual truth is largely dependent upon the accepted mores of science. Factual determinates are metaphorically symbolized by rock solid facts of logos. Thus my Orphan Stone is an errant pebble and likened to the youth that has gone astray. Separated from the flock I see myself as a living example of Jonathan Livingston Seagull, astray but living freely in the loving arms of mythos, unbound by the restrictions and limits imposed by logos.

> Astray is away from the correct path or direction, away from the right and good, as thought or behavior.[1]

Applying this definition to Lucy we find that astray projects a certain undesirable image for her. But I feel there is a deeper meaning. When the reality of the Rock is found in chaos, one suffers agonizing moments of loss and life altering conflict and disease. While logic dictates no retreat or refuge, the errant orphan sees it as an opportunity to activate the Way of the Stone. As an errant Orphan Stone I find it is a time for inner prosperity while others may yield to the formidable outer censorship imposed by staunch advocates of the rock. Such devotees risk not opening to the mystery of their own being.

The basic archetypal pattern of the orphan teaches us that one experiences suffering in two distinctly different Ways represented by the presence or absence of the Way of the Stone. First, one without the stone becomes a victim of causality in need of an outer savior. In the second way, the presence of the stone activates an inner creative force. The emergence of this force potentiates a new and yet unknown content of hidden meanings.

> The Stone refers to the ability of the integrated personality to perceive meaning and value in the most ordinary and even disagreeable of happenings. It is the change in the perceiving attitude, personality, which brings the transformation.[2]

Linus with a sigh of remorse declared, "I have so much to learn."

Reflecting upon the history of my life I discovered an individual whose fateful encounters with suffering were significantly influenced by the archetypal Orphan. Ironically I lived literally as an orphan from seven to eleven years of age. My childhood was missing.

When I became a physician, I learned there are certain essential scientific guidelines for establishing valid clinical practices. For instance, despite my serving the collective well, it always left me with the feeling that "something was missing." I accepted the modern paradigm of scientific medicine as the final word for all patients struggling with suffering, pain, disability of disease and death. At the same time I did not find a way to alleviate my own mysterious and troubling inner struggles and felt deeply the "problem of suffering." For me, the errant orphan, the successes of science were incomplete. My soul's yearning for wholeness remained ungratified. In this regard the wisdom of Jung resonated with me.

> Science is not indeed a perfect instrument but it is superb and an invaluable tool that works harm when it is taken as an end in itself. Science must serve; it errs when it usurps the throne. It obscures our insight only when it claims that the understanding it conveys is the only kind there is.[3]

I learned that many archetypal images are at play in the invisible world and that suffering is a necessary element for growth and development of all sentient beings. For instance, the Trickster is always at play. A mysterious creator of change, the trickster also has a redemptive value. At the appropriate times there is a mythic whispering in my ear, "Something is missing." The trickster is a daunting challenge to the ego whose full identity progressively comes to my awareness by introspection as mythos illumination.

My study of the writings of Carl Jung and Joseph Campbell gave me invaluable insights into the meaning of the Trickster's "wrecking ball" during the "cast astray" episodes happening in my atypical life. The repetitive and unsettling voice of the Trickster sent me on a lifelong quest that took me off the traditional path of the rock and catapulted me into the journey of the Stone.

I encountered numerous "kingdoms" of the Rock. I playfully refer to my experiences as my personal quest for the Holy Grail. Archetypically, I underwent the formative trials and tribulations of the quest and the suffering of an encroaching age.

I AM AN ORPHAN ALONE; NEVERTHELESS I AM FOUND EVERYWHERE.

Quest for the Stone

One day during high school, I, the youthful astray orphan, encountered the "knights of medicine" from the "Ivory Tower" of remedial medicine. Adorned with white vestments those wily knights of orthodoxy interrupted my typical adolescent reverie with their display of medical skills and amazing tales about the glory of winning adversarial jousts with disease and the thrill of conquering life threatening enemies within the body.

I was captivated. I realized this had something to do with my own destiny. It was an epiphany. Subsequently I embarked upon a quest for self-understanding guided by the innate calling of the Rock upon which medicine was built. I discovered that the Rock is a metaphor for professional fulfillment guided by the ability to communicate with medical terminology based on statistical valid "truths."

My epiphany initiated a series of twelve year cycles of learning. I accumulated medical skills by which to combat evil invaders from the domain of dreaded disease. My resume included positions as Air Force medical technician, medical school, internship, residence and medical

28

fellowship. Armed with therapeutic weapons, my sword forged and sharpened by determination, I took upon myself the persona of a novice knight and entered clinical tournaments enthusiastically anticipating the rigorous duties required of a fully fledged medical doctor. Medical school was a challenge but I was motivated by a "vision of saving the world."

My dream of becoming a "white knight of medicine" finally became a reality. I found myself quite skillful at yielding my shiny new blades. As time went by, however, it slowly, but persistently dawned upon me that all was not as I first supposed. I met with a painful frustration. A wall of ever deepening resistance obstructed my enchantment with medicine's ability to conquer the elusive suffering for those with intractable and chronic illness. These became my wounds that would not heal. As Percival failed to ask, "Whom does the Grail serve," my training had not prepared me to ask the Stone question, "What ails me."

I asked myself, why would any sane knight of the court of remedial medicine with a decorated career, a well pleased family, and bountiful material rewards have feelings of dissatisfaction? It seemed those typical gratifications of successful knighthood were symptomatically inadequate for fulfilling my need beyond some inner gratification.

Nevertheless, says Joseph Campbell, "Something in you, a divine urge compels one into the Quest. If one turns back, then the whole adventure goes out of life."[4]

This was the mythos answer to my continuing quest for "what was missing," so after my first twelve years of medical achievements I responded to the call for change and discovered new creative possibilities. It was a beckoning invitation from the Kingdom of Aerobics, an opportunity in Dallas, Texas. Perhaps, within that alternative domain of the rock, I could gain skill with alternative weapons by which to conquer the hidden dragon responsible for my inner distress as well as that of others.

Not so. There was no hint of a gratifying answer after one year of joyful participation in the daily jousts and conquests for wellness within this bastion of Aerobics. There was still "something missing."

One fortuitous day, while in this conscious lamentation, a messenger from a distant realm appeared with a scripted proposal. It was a pleading invitation to enter the service of a small kingdom in distress near a distant ocean, Santa Barbara, California. This monarch of third world diets was struggling in his combat against the siege posed by his powerful adversaries. Those orthodox authoritarians who felt it heresy to use primitive morsels in the treatment of the "wounds that will not heal" condemned his efforts.

My long discussions with this besieged monarch revealed in him a sharp mind filled with a wide range of expertise and medical war techniques, foreign to the beliefs and indoctrination of traditionally trained knights. This strange innovator, Nathan Pritikin, had accumulated that "expert" knowledge by his meticulous review of the medical and epidemiological texts which documented the validity of his therapeutic menu.

Although his expertise was alternative he was still a true disciple of the Rock. His depth of informational knowledge favorably altered a great deal of my initial skepticism. So I, the physician, submitted to a professional commitment to him, becoming his servant in this unorthodox court built on the rock I was urged to serve.

Pritiken's courtly challenge endowed me with the gift of a different kind of knowledge and expanded my combative valued skills and expertise in the battles with the shadowy "demons" of chronic disease. This meatless fare was declared unworthy for any noble warrior by orthodoxy, but my resolve was strengthened by the successful ongoing conquests in verbal combat with skeptics proving the validity for gorging themselves on an atypical high fiber and low fat, low cholesterol diet when added to the significant contribution of aerobic fitness. But the persistent anguish emanating from within the depths of my soul still announced "something was missing."

After two years of participation in this alternative version of the rock I felt my learning challenge had been fulfilled. For this reason I departed from the customary paths taken by other orthodox or alternative knightly seekers who built on the rock. I ventured forth on a solitary path into the dark forests of the non linear reality of my own venture into an alternative course. My quest for the treasured answer to something missing led me back to the citadel of Dallas.

The fame I earned during my turbulent adventures in the use of alternative remedies rewarded me with the shining jewels of prosperity, but also seduced me into deeds of debauchery and greed. Those fragile extravagances did not survive the storm of collective economic pestilence. As a consequence I was stripped of marital bliss and material wealth. Devastated I still reckoned that I possessed heretical fame gained from pursuing this alternative version of the rock. And...I still possessed a limited financial means to invest my efforts into a continued quest for that "something is missing."

My continuing journey brought me to a curiously weird village receptive of my equally curious identity as an alternative knight; Austin, Texas. My simple way of life in this flourishing community provided intriguing challenges for me and yielded abundant professional gratifications. The weapons in service to the rock for combat against the "wounds that would not heal" now included the magical gifts from natural sources as well as the physical and energetic therapies, forged tools yielded by the village blacksmiths. But "something was still missing."

I noted right away that a mysterious essence inhabited this village that was a Merlin-like presence. It was a place where the mask of distinction was various media reporting the by-words, "Keep Austin Weird." The market place for alternative health care bustled with the activity of a plethora of vendors announcing their esoteric wares, both domestic and foreign. The enchantment of several voices led me deeper and deeper into an awareness of a wide variety of spiritually-oriented phenomena. I encountered depth psychology. I was introduced to teachers of shamanism and I met guides leading me into sacred realms of esoteric wisdom. Their identities are chronologically listed in *Caduceus: A Physician's Quest for Healing.*

As my mission to discover alternative realities came under the influence of Merlin's spirit I gradually awakened to the existence of hidden possibilities residing in those darkened forests of the unconscious that might answer my persistent question, "something is missing." The sequential stages of my journey were initiated by those sages who reside in this alternate state of reality, teaching, and enticing me into the awareness of ancient mysteries. It was with trepidation colored by medical orthodoxy that I willingly, but skeptically, tread upon those beckoning paths.

My enchanted ventures into exotic realms revealed no magical resolution of my unrelenting agony. They all failed to redeem my sense of incompleteness. Out of frustration I undertook an explorative visit to the court of one of the most revered castles of orthodoxy founded upon the Rock of science: Harvard. My three day quest was anointed with a mysterious realization. Within this unlikely venue, "Spirituality and Healing," I experienced a spontaneous epiphany that touched the very ground of my heart and mind.

During my presence in that court one particularly interesting idea was presented by the leading magistrate. He presented the metaphor for healing as a three-legged stool; pharmacy, surgery and self-help. I couldn't believe my ears when he said that self-help included spirituality. Instead of soothing my wound, the shocking news thrown at me by the keeper of the rock cast me into further despair. Isolated by the darkest of the moments of confusion I encountered a vision of a mysterious presence.

Meeting the Friar

It was a youthful appearing friar garbed in the robe of a monk. He approached and stood before me. His untidy black hair and beard flowing down to his shoulders, he grinned from ear to ear. Brown eyes sparkling he said, "I am your brother from mythos." His touching announcement evoked a deeply numinous moment of unconditional love which intimately touched my heart. For the first time since my initiation into the quest of my longstanding agony, the "something is missing" spontaneously vanished.

He said, "White knight, you have devoted your life to your quest. Brother, you have traveled far and wide through many kingdoms founded on the Rock in search for the missing answer to your soul's question, "what ails me." I will guide you into the sacred space of mythos and you will now be shown a deeper meaning of life and certain hermetic wisdom."

In the flash of candescence I visualized a fourth leg to the magistrate's metaphor of the stool. I realized that the quest for something missing plus the question, "what ails me," had rewarded me with this candescent moment. I wondered where the friar had been all of my life. I realized that he had been lost among the guardians of the Rock only to appear when most needed in my life.

I realized that the revelation of the Friar is a vital key to subduing the ever present dragon question of "something is missing." Through his introspective vision the question, "what ails me" has a creative meaning. By activating my archetypal psyche I come to realize that I face a dilemma within my psyche rather than one dictated by outer causes and pursuit for remedies.

The invisible energy of the fourth leg opened me to the psychic reality that led me to the concept that the archetypal psyche contains the dynamism of all symbolic images. The instability of the three legged stool was transformed to a four legged stool and its inherent stability solved my problem of something was missing.

Subsequent company and increasing familiarity with the Friar aspect of my personality invited me into the art of simplicity and the deepening of heart centered feelings. The Friar's revelation introduced me to the healing value of the imagination. It revealed the value of metaphorical illumination, and my embrace with the creative feminine brought to me by the Stone wisdom.

I realized the outcome had not been possible as long as my knightly persona was dominated by the logos of the Rock. The irony is that my imagination had brought me to the compelling insight of the fourth leg which was the use of my imagination in healing; to contact the archetypal psyche with its symbolic images. Jung tells us about his similar experience which authenticates my own, "The play and counter play between personalities, No. 1 and No. 2, which has run through my whole life, has nothing to do with a 'split' or dissociation in the ordinary medical sense. On the contrary, it is played out in each individual. In my life No 2 has been of prime importance and I have always tried to make room for anything that wanted to come to me from within. He is a typical figure, but he is perceived only by a few. Most people's conscious understanding is not sufficient to realize that he is also what they are."[5]

Perhaps awareness, recognition and appreciation of the dynamics and workings of the Way of the Stone, may serve and have value for my fellow orphans as the Trickster becomes more active in their lives. The "cast astray" personality may discover, as I have, that. "The individual is nothing in collective, statistical terms, but everything from an inner standpoint."[6]

In our modern world that is a tremendously difficult viewpoint to champion. Attempting to communicate its implications for me as an errant orphan is the primary motivation for writing this book.

"The meaning of my existence is that life has addressed a question to me. Or, conversely, I myself am a question which is addressed to the world and I must communicate my answer, for otherwise I am dependent on the world's answer. That is a supra-personal task, which I acquire only after effort and with difficulty."[7]

Each collective entity metaphorically has an immune system with the functions of all the various types of cellular components which protect any particular body and maintain its life of sameness. This includes protective phagocytes which "kill" those cells identified as "gone astray."

It is in this errant "reality" that one encounters the mythology of Hermes, whose Wisdom speaks well to the solitary person.

WHO "KNOWS NEITHER FATHER NOR MOTHER?"

This metaphorical statement implies that one's identity or value is not exclusively a product of outer validation. Instead an individual submits to a spirit of independence, standing alone as one's inner truth; living one's myth. It is the hero's journey. It is an individual means of self-affirmation at the risk of collective rejection.

"The great truth: that each of us is a completely unique creature and that, if we are to give any gift to the world, it must come out of your own experience and fullness of your own potentialities, not someone else's. It is to be something out of one's own potential for experience, something that has never been and could never have been experienced by anyone else."[8]

From Joseph Campbell I learned that myth serves a transformative function which opens the world to the dimension of archetypal messages, to the mystery that underlies all forms. Subsequently I will address my interface with the transcendent mystery through my loss of Kyle. Mythology consists of stories about the wisdom of life which help put my soul in touch with the innate creative dynamism yearning to be revealed and acted out during his life and at his death.

I realize the Way of the Orphan Stone is the primary myth predicting my previous fateful encounters and the continued unfolding drama of my life. It charges my old age with meaning and purpose and at the same time creates a nontraditional, "gone astray" symbolizing my attitude in relationship to the problem of suffering by diminishing the grip of victimhood upon my soul. A mythos meaning for Kyle's life and death is my ultimate challenge that tests my devotion to the Wisdom of the Stone.

CHAPTER 5

WISDOM OF THE STONE

Kyle's loss, treading near the valley of death, engendered a level of grief which could easily have overwhelmed me and made the remaining days of my life tragically miserable, ever desiring to regain what is lost. I have heartfelt compassion for all the individuals who must endure similar tests of fire, feeling isolated and abandoned; orphaned.

I too feel the heaviness of the burden of suffering and the victim's frantic heartbeat. There is wisdom to be learned and I submit to its call. I place my suffering within the circle of Stones representing Hermes. I sacrifice it to the archetype of transformation as my friar aspect offers devotion to the Way of the Stone which speaks to my heart and rattles my bones.

Golden Treatise

Understand ye Sons of wisdom, the stone declares: Protect me, and I will protect thee; give me my own, that I may help you.

— The Golden Treatise of Hermes.

As I reflected upon the Golden Treatise I was compelled to amplify its content because it represents the essential key to understanding the Wisdom of the Stone.

It is during such overwhelming circumstances that the archetypal level of my soul is stimulated. I feel the grip of the deep wisdom of the Stone nearby. Emerging awe inspires psychical images whose symbolic significance imparts a candescent impact upon my soul. Hermetic wisdom shows me the Way of the Stone and gives me the sacred insight that metaphorically the Rock and Stone are fundamentally different.

The lessons of the Rock are from the ordinary world. The Rock is about the collective; the flock. For collective good Moses drew water from the Rock. The gifts of the Stone are from a non-ordinary world, but are nevertheless real. Concretely understood, they are worthless while symbolically they impart value and have creative meanings. The nature of the Stone involves archetypal images of an inner process. For the individual good Hermes draws water from the Stone.

Hermes declared he was "the friend of anyone who was alone; of everyone who is separated from the flock."[1]

Hermes serves as my friend and counselor of my archetypal orphan who leads me to the discovery of the "precious Stone" within. Hermes is my teacher and guide mediating between the Orphan and the Stone.

"The name Hermes is derived from the Greek word herm, the name of a pile of stones marking a boundary. His mythological function is indicated by his name—hermeneutics, extracting the hidden meaning beyond the ordinary boundaries of human understanding."[2]

The innate healing wisdom of the Hermetic circle of Stones is thus defined as the ability to candidly craft one's own truth. For only "what is true will heal us." Therefore it is a question of personal integrity. It is an inner voice arising within oneself. One has a strange feeling of certainty about the right thing to do, no matter what the collective code says. Ethical codes are treated with a kind of natural wisdom that is not limited to the black and white distinctions given by them. It is a basic genuineness that comes from the depths of the individual soul.

On balance, we who travel from east to west and between north and south know the benefit derived from the "truths" of the Rock. I know that my continued physical survival in this world and the benefits I have derived from "common" education are testimonies to the value of that "truth" of the Rock. The Stone gave me uncommon wisdom through the Friar.

To receive that wisdom I must honor and understand the creative role of symbols at play when adversity challenges the conditional happiness of my "good times." To embrace the creative role of suffering I must understand that it is an enigma to my ego who must protect me <u>at all costs</u> against irrational happenings that threaten attachments to the desired status quo. The Stone contains the marvelous secret of the individual. It remains the treasure of the lonely person.

I nevertheless have learned to survive by existing in a world of rational contradictions and unpredictable happenings because I seek understanding over the glory of greatness. I asked myself if this natural dilemma of life, which leads or casts me astray, primarily serves to stimulate some cultural demand for coping with suffering or some pharmaceutical response to serve the pleasure principle. I wanted to know if it might serve me in my heroic quest for some understanding of my soul.

We all seek protection of some sort seldom realizing that all beloved archetypes are reciprocal.

Protection

Protect me, and I will protect thee

Any worthwhile understanding of the Stone is unveiled by appropriate sacrifices. Literal meanings, spiritual diversions, and absolute dependence upon mundane values defend against discovery of my Stone. I realized that something was happening to my thinking when I discovered I had been exposed to the Way of the Stone.

"Well, our thinking then lacks all leading ideas and sense of direction emanating from them. We no longer compel our thoughts along a definite track, but let them float, sink or rise according to their specific value. Thinking is sort of "inner acts of the will," and its absence necessarily leads to an "automatic play of ideas" (images)."[3]

I found the experience of those "inner acts of will" is absolutely crucial for interfacing with the Wisdom of the Stone. Participation in the mythos of Stone consciousness is typically aborted by the modern mind. The mundane world is conditioned to think exclusively in logical terms, claiming that myths are untrue. Meanwhile those inner "truths" which remain unconscious must nonetheless surface in other ways. Thus, we suffer. The Stone initiated me into the mythos of creative imagination.

I AM HIDDEN IN THE INNER MOST SOUL OF MEN.
I AM MORTAL FOR EVERYONE, YET I AM NOT
TOUCHED BY THE CYCLE OF EONS."

Creative imagination in healing: "This activity with images introduces the term archetype or primordial idea. An idea which differs from all other concepts in that it is not a datum of experience serving the intellectual, logos activity of mind. The dynamism of the Stone includes the mystery existing beyond those mental evaluations attached to concrete matter. For that mythic function the soul is receptive for archetypal images, underlying principle of all experience, and the vitality they bring to the diversity of mundane or sacred experiences."[4]

Creative imagination is a tool of introspection. When one suffers, the immediate reaction is to ask, "What is happening to me?" That is the beginning of reflection. Is it a road protected by the Rock whereby one suffers from symptoms to be alleviated and the effects of outer causalities to be cured? Or is it to be the protection of the Stone in harmony with an inner voice calling for a different type of wisdom?

I find that the protection of the Stone is not an act of defending against some personal enemy. It is an art of maintaining and participating in the wisdom of mythos on the inside while remaining silent in the world of the mundane. This is a way of seeming less foolish, or protecting others from contents of the unconscious before they are ready for the challenge.

The protection the Stone reciprocates. It arises from the spontaneous transformation revealed in archetypal images which manifest in visions, dreams, active and passive imagination. It is the Stone that conveys a creative message emanating from the soul in the form of an essential image. In other words, the image-making power of the stone derives from assessing the center of one's being, and is not limited to the intellectual function of logos (the absence of mythos) favored by a superficial sense of identity.

One's unique orphan state may initially identify with a deity and arrogantly assume a personal power, believing to be able to manipulate images for achieving spiritual wishes, a medical cure, personal betterment or acquisition of some other magical effect. The Stone responds to neither magical effects nor evangelistic zeal. The Stone protects the orphan psyche from possession by grandiosity, negative inflation, or alienation.

One's feeling of being different may prompt a loss of interest in society, i.e., reclusive living as the hermit or the chronically homeless. The individual experience of "being astray" without the protection of the Stone may also foster an estrangement from society where emptiness, despair, and alienation may lead to violent reactivity. The Stone is a source of nurturing for the hunger of my soul, answering my question, "what is missing?" It protects me from those symptoms typical of a starving soul.

The customary sense of "having roots" implies that there is some form of tribal or societal creed holding forth a successful belief system thus producing a well-functioning tribe or society. But, "a loss of roots and lack of tradition causes collective neuroses and hysteria calls for collective solutions, which consists in loss of liberty and terrorization. Where rational materialism holds sway, states tend to develop less into prisons than into lunatic asylums."[5]

The Stone provides relevant myths or symbolic images, which are protective, because its wisdom contains a profound awareness of my archetypal roots. "The Hermetic philosophy regarded the archetypes as inalienable components of the empirical world picture. He was not yet so demented by the object that he could ignore the palpable presence of the eternal idea, the archetype."[6]

Give Me My Own

The role of submission for the process of death and transformation is an essential element of the journey. The mysterious aspect of the symbols within ordinary perceptions is the essential agent activating an inner source of archetypal energy beyond workings of personal will. Mythos uniquely yields its mystery by way of symbols, metaphor, and mythology. Sometimes an entire process can be revealed in a few words. "Give me my own" is such a phrase. The wisdom of the Stone demands respect and devotion to its process, the journey.

But the orphan must humbly realize, "If the wrong man uses the right method, the right means work in the wrong way. The method is merely the path, the direction taken by man; the way he acts is the true expression of his nature. If it ceases to be this, the method is no more than an affectation serving only the goal of self deception. This is in sharp contrast to our belief in the right method irrespective of the man who applies it."[7]

Culturally driven processes fit the needs of the "statistical human." They are indeed well served, but the precious stone of mythos remains out of sight. The need for a "cure" is the sufferer's attempt to find resolution on the same level as the perceived illness. Reason must seek the solution in some rational, logical way. It is incapable of creating a symbol because the symbol is irrational.

In contrast, "healing," defined by the Stone, does not exist on the same level as the illness. It seeks a symbol whose truth reveals a transformational, creative value in adversity. The Stone speaks to the mystery of mythos which ultimately heals and transforms the suffering. It is archetypal of the eternal Trickster in thinking. Mythos is a nasty plague for logos of linear thinking.

"The fate of Asclepius, from Greek mythology, is that curing someone who was meant to die would lead to the healer's own death in place for the one cured. Asclepius brought Hippolytus back to life through his healing power, but transcended what was meant to be and thus Asclepius himself was killed by Zeus for challenging divine decree."[8]

The fate of Asclepius exemplifying the mystery of the stone is a faithful enactment of a mythological dynamic. It means that curing anyone who was "meant to die" (transform) would lead to the healer's own death. Metaphorically it means that the healer is no longer an active participant in the process unlike the physician's typical savior role in today's practice of logical therapies using collective determination and remedial action to prevent physical death at all costs.

"The right reaction to a symptom may as well be a welcoming rather than laments and demand for remedies for the symptom is the first herald of an awakening psyche which will not tolerate any more abuse. Because the symptoms lead to the soul the cure may also lead away from the soul. To get rid of the symptom means to deprive one of the chance to gain what may have been of the greatest value."[9]

Individual submission is the gift allowing something altogether strange to rise up to confront him or her from the hidden depths of the soul. It is initially experienced as forbidden, such as my initial reaction to Kyle's death. But, in the process of acceptance I have gained access to the sources of psychical life which initiates the healing process. As an orphan my otherwise "rock" solid rational understanding alone added nothing to the healing of my grief. I cannot logically redeem my grief, but rather draw it forth from the stone through mythos.

If my choice is to serve the Rock to the exclusion of the Stone then I risk losing an opportunity of redemption from my grief. This great "sin" represents not giving the symbolic vitality its due. The archetypal content of my grief will be rationalized and put at the disposal of traditional ways of thinking by diagnostic codes and conscious morality. Although that thinking is rationally correct, it fails to grasp the true nature of my suffering as a unique individual.

As you may conclude, the Way of the Orphan Stone leads me to an atypical process outside those parameters which define usual and customary. My quest has led me to a marvelous but lonely place where archetypal images are giving me messages of healing symbolism concerning the divine nature of Kyle's life and death.

My Stone says: "Do not squander my hermetic wisdom by investing in the talisman and amulets with magical powers in my name; some concretizing actions through which to manipulate outer reality; some mesmerizing activity serving the exoteric alchemist or some Sorcerer's magic. Let them all have their own. Rather than serve some profane advantage favored by the orthodox disciples of the Rock give me my own meaning. So that the infinite mystery may reveal itself as an inner creative, redeeming wisdom uniquely mine."

Neither does The Wisdom of Hermes qualify as an article of faith such as derived from the Biblical Old and New Testaments or the Koran. The following tale derived from an ancient text reveals the substance of that premise.

"The initiatory experiences Hermes sponsors as he guides our souls between the realms, bringing the dreams of more than reason. Where we go with dreams, the messages, the gold coins of Hermes purse, is up to us. The fable maker Babrius has him given voice to the dilemma and possibility in following story:

> A stonemason made a marble Herm for sale
> And men came up to bid. One wanted it
> For a tombstone, since his son was lately dead.
> A craftsman wanted to set it up as a god
> It was late, and the stonemason had not sold it yet
> So he said, "Come back tomorrow and look at it again."
> He went to sleep and lo! In the gateway of dreams
> Hermes stood and said, "My affairs now hang in the balance,
> Do not make me one thing or another, dead man or god."[10]

The Stone, the soul, and the Holy Grail in the reality of mythos are symbolically one and the same. The Stone as the soul is not a lifeless material substance to be used for divination, curing ills or prolonging longevity, nor does it qualify as a foundation for a religion. Instead it carries the natural wisdom of Sophia.

The inner reaches of the soul are aroused during circumstances of suffering; a deeper source of wisdom is activated. Awe inspiring images arise spontaneously from the archetypal psyche whose symbolic significance imparts a candescent affect upon the orphaned individual appearing in dreams and during various techniques of active imagination. It is a mystical experience when compared to the prevailing logos bound view of reality.

"The culture-creating mind is ceaselessly employed in devising formulas to explain the forces of nature and to express them in the best ways possible. But, when directed thinking is no longer adaptive then psychic energy descends into the unconscious and there attaches to an unconscious focus. The process of fantasy thinking, mythos, gives us the potential to listen to its message and release an unconscious creative impulse of the "stone" into a living experience."[11]

That I May Help You

How is one served by this fortuitous announcement? The answer is revealed in the wounding healing paradox of the Trickster. The mythological origins for our miseries which we must bear include a complementary process of healing. "The one that wounds is the one who heals." Is it possible to realize that suffering serves the ontological purpose of imparting wisdom?

"There is the Greek legend of the hero Telephos, wounded by Achilles in the upper thigh with the wound that would not heal. An oracle declares, "He that wounds shall also heal!" and after a long and painful quest Telephos finds Achilles and is healed. Or according to another reading, the cure is effected by the weapon: the remedy being scraped off the point and sprinkled in the wound."[12]

Jung's basic thesis was that the Way of the Stone is fully embraced as a benefactor for a very few. The forbidden or discarded experiences of life as defined by the Rock are rejected, but become a source of wisdom for seekers of the Stone. The associated candescence illuminates a wholeness of each personality, becoming the person one truly is. Candescence, according to its definition, requires candidness or certain honesty with oneself.

Said another way is not wearing "authentic amour," thus suffering the consequences of programmed, single minded, monotonous efficiency of bureaucratic formalism, and collective conformity has its consequences. The instinct to follow the herd is so strong that one cannot pull away. The subsequent depression, irritability, insomnia, painful joints, headaches, rise in blood pressure, disturbance in heart and intestinal functions are therapeutic gold for the pharmaceutical industry. Viewing the movie, "Joe Versus the Volcano" with Tom Hanks and Meg Ryan provides a dramatic display of this scenario.

"It's the problem of the wasteland—people living life inauthentic ally, living not their life but the life that's put on them by the society."[13]

The paradoxical nature of Hermes is that he is an active facilitator of the Stone process, a teacher and guide mediating between the Stone and the Orphan. On the other hand, as a trickster he is the initiator of the process. He is also the thief who steals security blankets and provides a rocky road on which to travel. As I reflect upon my son's death I am coaxed into introspection and relish a comfort in reflecting upon a Charles Schulz *Peanuts* cartoon:

Linus says to Charlie Brown, "Look Charlie Brown, you have fears and you have frustrations—am I right? Of course I am right! So what you need is a blanket to soak up your fears and frustrations."
Charlie says, "I don't know—I think most of life's problems are too complicated to be solved with a spiritual blotter."

The mystery of the Stone manifests the archetypal Hermes as the agent of transformation, the Trickster, who steals our treasured "security blankets" and changes the course of life for better or worse. In any of one of its many personifications is always in transit from the human world of logos and the divine reality of mythos.

Charlie, true to the Orphan Stone, adds a profound bit of wisdom related to the orthodox "isms" of our extremely complex world. I personally concur with Charlie's statement as I explore the mythos of Kyle's death. In

45

the spirit of the Way of the Stone I am obligated to propose that the usual problems of life are not fully contained by a single absolute ideology or creed. As logos they represent a wide range of discrepant, contradictory truths, with each being accepted as the truth based strictly on the logos of faith. As an orphaned trickster facing the loss of his beloved son I candidly wonder outside the conformity of any "ideological blotter."

CHAPTER 6

THE TRICKSTER

W hen first seeing this picture of The Jackal I was struck with an ominous sense of awe. My immediate thought was, "this is Kyle's trickster! I was then given his identity, Tsakali. One of Kyle's closest companions gave the following insight, "In the past Kyle

had a stealthy, mystical way about him. In addition, he was very intelligent but kept mostly to himself. But during the last year I witnessed a personality change coinciding with the emergence of Tsakali. He began to be more socially active and assertive in expressing himself. It caused me to ponder what was his role in Kyle's divine drama.

Introduction

Appreciating the full imaginative potential of the archetypal force we call it the Trickster. It is a basic and essential condition for anyone entering the Way of the Stone. This champion of chaos appears prominently in the mythology and folklore of nearly every culture in the world. It is a role which disrupts the logical values of control, balance and order. It strikes terror in the heart of the righteous.

Therefore, the ruling advocates of traditional logos, the rock, demonize the Trickster because it paradoxically threatens the integrity of their cherished boundaries. A consequence whereby the one "cast astray" is determined to be a victim. It is illogical to understand otherwise.

47

It is generally true that our time-bound fear, driven by linear thinking demonizes the role of the trickster and empathetically deifies the role of the victim who "suffers" from the burden of so-called "involuntary" tribulations. Therefore, a major portion of the energy we expend by living in fear is completely consumed by avoiding or diminishing risk, and out of desire persistently striving to overcome the consequences of unwanted chaos. While serving the instincts for survival and the hopeful desires of the ego, each of those obsessions subtract from the transforming capacity for mythos reflection and consequent revelation. Thus a trouble maker, the trickster, is activated.

To understand otherwise is to embrace the creativity demanded by this archetypal image whereby one must depart from logos and enter the imaginative world of mythos. Worldwide mythologies provide us with fascinating tales which dramatize the nature of this instigator of mischief who champions the force for creative change. It is the "devilish" image which tricks us into the awareness of paradox, the knowledge of "good" and "evil." When the soul announces a call for creative change, healing or deflation of grandiosity, it manifests the "pathological" activity of a trickster.

"The trickster character appears in the narratives of many Native people throughout North America as well as much of the rest of the world. Even in our own culture people catch glimmers of the trickster in the characters of Br'er Rabbit, wily Coyote, and Buggs Bunny. It is difficult to pin down the trickster to any fixed set of characteristics or given forms. Part of his/her attraction is in defiance of classification and analysis. Sometimes the trickster appears as human, sometimes as animal. The most popular animal forms trickster takes are coyote, raven, and hare. The trickster plays tricks and is the victim of tricks, the trickery of such stories extends as well to symbolic play regarding cultural forms, rules, and worldview."[1]

To embrace the value of the trickster, the source of our greatest yearnings and fears, is a central and fundamental necessity for the livelihood of the Stone. Its imperatives can plunge us into the experience of dismemberment and separation, such as my spontaneous devastated feeling upon initially hearing of Kyle's death. Subsequently, I have placed my suffering upon the altar of mythos. Thus I embark upon the Way of the Stone which transforms the trickster into the redeemer as well as the one who wounds.

"A curious combination of typical trickster motifs can be found in the alchemical figure of Mercurius; for instance, his fondness for sly jokes and malicious pranks, his powers as a shift shaper, his dual nature, his exposure to all kinds of tortures and last but not least—his approximation to the figure of the savior. This association is confirmation of the mythological truth that as an agent of healing it is the sufferer that takes away the suffering."[2]

Previously in this book I have given the Trickster its due by suggesting that it defies the fixed boundaries given to us by logos. The established "wrapping of words" around the definition of things that happen to us or established factual truth encounters its nemesis, the Trickster. In the succeeding chapters I have continued discussing the repeated events which have acquainted me with the full dynamic force of the Trickster.

In the Preface I introduce Jung's "misfit" cornerstone and its creative consequences. Next I present the Adversity of Kyle's death which seeks redemption through my devotion to the Way of the Stone. I further introduce the Errant Orphan who is cast or led astray from the "right and good" values founded on the rock. I provide my personal encounter with the trickster by the telling of the knight's long quest for the "something missing." In the latest chapter I am given the Wisdom of the Stone, the Trickster personified by Hermes. Therefore it is obvious I am willing to concede that the Trickster is the culprit who instigates the foolish wisdom vital for the Way of the Orphan Stone.

Part One, the Forbidden

From the standpoint of my logos' capacity to understand the most *forbidden* personal event possible was the termination of Kyle's physical presence in my life. It is critically more acceptable for the reverse scenario to have occurred. During the initial trauma I refused to give the Trickster my blessings or forgiveness. It was inconceivable for me to give any positive value to the pain inflicted upon me. The Trickster became my tormenter. I knew that there was a reconcilable conflict associated with my anger toward the Trickster. In reference to Kyle's death I also knew the Stone was yet to be discovered.

Of the three previous major initiations throughout the course of my life, none reached this magnitude of intensity. The story of my last ritual, "Initiation of the Elder" is described in *Caduceus: A Physician's Quest for Healing.* In it I described how I programmed my bilateral knee replacement as a sacred ritual thus introducing the Elder aspect of my personality into consciousness. I experienced a falling away of personal attachments and opened up further to the mystery of archetypes. Subsequent initiations have amplified my participation in the dynamic of the unconscious and motivated my esoteric explorations into the Way of the Orphan Stone.

Facing the full spectrum of the Trickster, including the acceptance of redemptive value, is a daunting task for it demands introspection, i.e., inspecting the inner processes of the soul. This irreversible force strives for candidly facing one's inner truth, and at the same time confronts the immovable obstacles imposed by the outer Guardians of orthodoxy where good intentions serve outer adaptation and social duty.

Each of us then may ask: is it possible for me to "lend unto Caesar what is Caesar's" and at the same time discover my "precious stone". Awareness of the cost, risk, and potential benefit for the solitary individual are factors which aid in sorting out any answer. The consequence of introspection is no more or no less than that of "becoming conscious," which is the unending purpose of adversity.

Costly to All

"The way is not without danger. Everything good is costly and development of the personality is one of the most costly of all things. It is a matter of saying yea to oneself, of taking oneself as the most serious of tasks, of being conscious of everything one does and keeping it constantly before one's eyes in all its dubious aspects—truly a task that taxes us to the utmost."[3]

I remember on several occasions when a patient would announce, "I would do anything to be free of my illness!" I responded "really?"

Approximately describing the illness free personality he or she would need to become, the steadfast response was, "I could never be that person, I would rather die" or "Lord *forbid* that should happen to me."

"The Stone refers to the ability of the integrated personality to perceive meaning and value in the most ordinary and even disagreeable of happenings. *It is the change in the perceiving attitude, personality, which brings the transformation.*"[4]

This persistent resistance to change common to all sentient beings gives birth to the Trickster. Willful intent to defend against chaos is both a powerful force for accomplishment and equally powerful mechanism for failure. As with all experience it is not immune from paradox. The Trickster insists upon it. I can attest personally that the failures throughout my life have transformed me while my successes have gratified my state of grandiosity temporarily keeping me attached to my "trophies."

In retrospect I am grateful for experiencing both the pleasurable "stuff" of willful efforts and the gift of subsequent failures that fate planned for me. The value of that paradoxical combination is incomprehensible for the vast majority of those whose primary measure of happiness is determined by the criteria of material acquisitions.

I was a guest at a birthday party. Most of the twelve attendees ranged in age from 35 to 50 years. At age 66 I sat listening to everyone else who relished the benefits of their successful entrepreneurial achievements. Four were current patients in my medical practice.

To break the ice, our creative hostess initiated questions meant to stimulate and entertain all present. For example, she asked, "What was your most embarrassing moment?" We each responded to the other's answers with a mix of laughter and admiring amazement. The next question: "What has been the most inspiring experience in your life?" Playing the social game, we shared common reactions as each in turn responded to her queries.

Then it came to my turn. I thought of many inspirational examples from my life, but the question was for the one "most" inspiring or pivotal event. I proceeded to relate the details of my painful financial struggle to avoid bankruptcy. I told about having to face the evidence and proof of my failures, economically as well as personally, with a failed marriage. Adding the final twist, I recounted the sale of my last symbol of success; a diamond Rolex President's watch in order to finance a move to Austin, Texas. It was to be a new beginning.

I sensed that my heartfelt presentation had an apocalyptic affect for those present, their jovial demeanor vanishing like water extinguishing a flame. Stunned silence reigned for long minutes. The hostess attempted to rescue the moment. She directed the question to the next person in rotation. But… the damage had been done. The party was over. Peace, harmony and joy were shocked by the Trickster. The Trickster had surfaced casting a shadow upon the thrones of shining successes touching upon the forbidden fear motivating their compensatory values and efforts for success.

The "grandiosity" of their cherished personas threatened, they no longer wanted to play. Those four who had been patients I never saw again. The lesson I learned from this experience; when the uninvited Trickster manifests, we all suffer consequences. I concluded that one can be perceived as either wise or foolish depending upon whom one is speaking to at the moment.

> The greatest obstacle to being heroic is the doubt whether one might not be going to prove one's self a fool; the true heroism is to resist the doubt, and profoundest wisdom is to know when it ought be resisted, and when to be obeyed.
>
> — Nathanial Hawthorne, "The Birth Date of Romance," 1852

I also concluded that stepping upon the mystical path is initiated by sacrifice and suffering from the standpoint of the ego. It is rarely undertaken voluntarily. Any irreversible attachment to conditional happiness and fixed aversion to suffering are both obstacles for discovering the Wisdom of the Stone.

The Trickster introduces the forbidden thing, the dreaded burden meant to initiate the soul into the Way of the Stone. Consequently the personality begins to perceive reality as a subtle Candescence, a symbol for consciousness. The symptoms become harbingers for creative inner change rather than solely a plea for palliative remedy or coping techniques offered by dominate collective paradigms of modern science and "secular" religions.

Risky for Most

Previously discussed, ordinary reductive thinking is rigidly fixed for the vast logical majority. Thinking is dominated by the terminology of logos. Popular acceptance of a mythos reality is not intellectually feasible, except in poetry and art. Ordinarily an individual feels well served with the containment offered by their status quo life style and the absoluteness of causality. To consider otherwise is forbidden. But…there are two realities.

The entrance into the Way of the Stone has its guardians, fear and desire. The obscure, unordinary, mythic reality of the Stone is a threat to be feared by the ideological and scientific bastions protecting the "so called" sane personality. The tunnel vision of religion and science are absolutely dependent upon faith and/or so called facts. Therefore, the precious stone as a "myth" has no practical value and is potentially dangerous. Rock solid attachment to the logic of knowledge closes the gateway leading to the wisdom of the Stone. That happens because we are attached to the logical explanations for what happens to us in life rather than risk giving priority to the uniqueness of individual experience.

Risk is further defined by the phrase, "To eat or be eaten." This is an appropriate metaphor expressing the paradoxical potentials experienced from encounters with the animal nature of the Trickster. To be symbolically eaten means the onslaught of instinct takes one into the jaws of death or psychosis. In other words, if the "ecstatic-fantasy" does not transform your personality, it may metaphorically eat you.

Lion eating the man
Bagdad Museum 720 BC

"The onslaught of instinct becomes the experience of divinity, provided man does not succumb to it and follow it blindly, but defends his humanity against the animal nature of the divine power. It is a fearful thing to fall into the hands of a living god.[5]

The experience of fantasy is then for ecstasy only, and does not serve the progressive maturation of the psyche, redemption by Way of the Stone. When an individual falls under control of archaic fantasy figures, adaptation to life itself is disturbed and "so-called" accidents tend to happen. Nothing is gained ontologically since the psychic energy of the fantasy does not serve candescence or initiation. The individual has become stuck in an all enveloping phantasmagoria with runaway destructive possession, psychosis, or death.

When that happens, a transformational challenge becomes toxic for the fragile personality, truly forbidden. Those who are chronically overwhelmed by the things that happen to him or her revert to a childhood state of dependency; an orphan forever seeking an equivalent for mother or father to give them protective refuge.

Rather than entering the Way of the Stone, the individual victim state of being becomes attached to an individual or collective entity for protection. These orphans seek and feel well served by refuge within a meditative transcendent experience, a religious containment, a secular group sanctuary, or an attachment to an individual who does not challenge or threaten the existing personality.

The candescent Way to the Stone is closed and the Trickster labeled demonic; paradox denied. As a consequence devotees of the Rock forever judge it as the deceptive serpent in the Garden of Eden whose atrocious deed casts mankind's state of innocence into one of suffering from the knowledge of "good and evil."

Jung interestingly related his concept of God to the archetype of the Trickster during an interview printed in *Good Housekeeping*, Dec. 1961: "To this day God is the name by which I designate all things which cross my willful my path violently and recklessly, all things which upset my subjective views, plans, and intentions and change the course of my life for better or worse."

For those individuals who rigidly believe the Trickster represents only the evil Satan, the Way of the Orphan Stone is forbidden. Therefore it is condemned as heretical. Metaphorically, the innocent sheep which has separated from the flock must be saved by the good shepherd or it will be eaten by hungry "wolves." The collective rational mind labels the interplay with images insane and forbidden, except in children, poets, artists, prophets, saints and the creativity of madness, of unresolved suffering.

The "protection of the stone" is placed at risk or deleted by rituals which include the use of substances and/or artificial induction with paraphernalia into a state of ecstatic eroticism. Such encounters carry the risk of being overwhelmed by death or persistent psychosis that the individual may be "eaten" by the dark side of altered states. They are ill advised to open the forbidden portal into a hellish journey of impossible tasks given by the Way of the Orphan Stone unless assisted by visible and invisible helpers attuned to the mythos version of reality.

In reference to the use of devices including drugs Joseph Campbell advises, "The mechanically induced mystical experience is what you have here. I have attended a number of psychological conferences dealing with this whole of the difference between the mystical experience and a psychological crack-up. The difference is that one who cracks up is drowning in the water in which the mystic swims. You have to be prepared for that experience."[6]

The Thread from Ariadne provides orientation within the process and prevents one from getting lost in the labyrinth of the archetypal mystery. It then possesses the participant and becomes an addiction or fixation risk. It is to be done only when facilitated by a professional director, Jungian psychologist or ritual elder as a guide who "knows" the boundaries and firmly grasps the dangers.

Obviously, the perceived value of the precious Stone is subject to the diversity of human interpretation. While the conscious function of the majority is bound exclusively to those perceptions available to the senses and intellect, there are those individuals whose archetypal pattern or personality contains an aptitude for constructively engaging the mystery of mythos.

Just as there is a category of humans who are physically gifted and athletically successful, sports come easier for them compared to us less physically endowed. Jung provides insights into the innate aspects of personality basic to understanding the issue of individual aptitude, psychologically.[7]

Beneficial for the Receptive Few

"In the same way that the body needs food, the soul needs to know the meaning of its existence, not just any meaning, but the meanings of those images and ideas which reflect its nature and which originate in the unconscious."[8]

Those who lack the numinous experience engendered by ingestion of mystical food might ask if the "obesity of logos" results from exclusive overconsumption of intellectually "rich" foods provided by logos. Consequently, the mythos appetite for meaning is never fully appeased. Something is always missing. The hungry soul is never completely satiated. An incessant craving may manifest in alcohol and drug addictions, intellectual elitism, or metaphorically by the way people over-consume, obsessively moving from one material craving to another. Meanwhile the hungry soul remains unsatiated. Thus, we suffer.

The seeds of the Stone have not fallen on receptive, fertile ground. To be unreceptive is not a weakness or failure, but a state of consciousness whose "rock solid" perspective forbids receptivity. The Trickster is forever an adversary to be combated. As previously stated, this premise of the "very few" exists in the modern era because the extraverted mentality present in the vast majority of people excludes mythos thinking as being pertinent to the fateful realities actually imposed by life. There is a mythos drought; something is missing.

"If you contemplate your lack of fantasy, of inspiration and inner aliveness, which you feel as sheer stagnation and a barren wilderness and impregnate it with the interest born of your own of the alarm of your inner death, then something can take shape in you, for your inner emptiness conceals just as great a fullness if only you allow it to penetrate into you. If you prove receptive to this "call of the wild," the longing for fulfillment will quicken the sterile wilderness of your soul as rain quickens the bare earth."[9]

In addition, the demand for instant-gratification "fast foods" negates any nurturing by an ongoing process, i.e., the Way of the Stone. As previously noted the education of the vast majority in our culture is dependent upon logos bound determinates. The experience of becoming more candid about one's true identity is taboo. But, for the receptive few, self-knowledge comes from interfacing with a mystery, as mythos, beyond the limits imposed by causal determinates and emotional reactivity.

The evolving human intellect has over time produced a multitude of religious-spiritual, philosophical, and scientific means to interpret and respond to the problem of suffering. From the menu of logos there are many potential "truths" which interface with painful challenges. The Way of the Orphan Stone is only one way and not the absolute way. It is therefore invalid for the vast majority who exclusively believe in the absoluteness of their way. It does redeem the uniqueness of a very few responsive orphans for whom the labor pains of suffering signal a rebirth.

When the archetypal Stone is activated it is a call to stand alone with one's own truth. One escapes the confines of absolute normality becoming one of the few receptive souls who venture into the garden present within the depths of each soul. It is a submission to the process of personal transformation by accepting that the Way of the Stone is an attempt to break through your subjectivity and heal you. This is accomplished by giving the pain inflicted by the trickster a positive value for "breaking of the shell that encloses your understanding."

> "And the woman spoke, saying, Tell us of pain.
> And he said:
> Your pain is the breaking of the shell
> That encloses your understanding.
> Even as the stone of the fruit must break
> That its heart may stand in the sun, so you must know pain.
> And should you keep your heart in wonder
> At the daily miracles of your life, your pain
> Would not seem less wondrous than your
> Joy."
> — Gibran, Kahlil, *The Prophet*, p. 52

Part Two, Redeemed

I AM HIDDEN IN THE INNER MOST SOUL OF MEN.

Freeing what is hidden.
The solitary creative soul,
Thereby
Standing alone as your truth,
Becoming the person you are.

This realization stimulates a process which Carl Jung termed individuation. Joseph Campbell interpreted it as "following your bliss, truly feeling alive." The Christian announces it as a state of "grace." Oriental thinking reveals it as being either "in the Tao" or Buddha consciousness.

Jung taught, "Every great experience in life, every profound conflict, evokes the accumulated treasure of images and brings about their inner constellation. But they become accessible to consciousness only when the person possesses so much self awareness that he or she reflects on what is experienced instead of living it blindly. In which case, he or she actually lives the myth and the symbol without knowing it."[10]

Jung acknowledged this source of "truth" as the spontaneous experience of synchronicity, active imagination, fantasy thinking, visions, dreams, and the transcendent function of the symbol, all seen in mythology of the Trickster. Without this mythological, archetypal awareness you are not effectively dedicated to standing alone as your truth, becoming the person who by name is a "precious stone."

The symbolic Stone represents what Jung called the transcendent function.[11] It facilitates a transition from one attitude to another. It is an act of redemption. It brings dreams and symbolic fantasy levels to a new way of life which can suddenly lead to a new attitude. A previously unknown quality renews the personality with a life-enhancing energy. The forbidden act, "the wounding," initiates a venture into another dimension, or sacred space, where one may experience the presence of archetypal images, the personality transformed, while in heterogeneous time, "untouched by eons."

The broad definition for redeem basically means freedom, liberation from guilt, escaping from bondage, or release from an obligation of some sort. The word "redeem" therefore refers to three separate contexts: salvation from sinfulness, relief from a financial or other obligation, or release from emotional attachment.[12]

The Stone, as a redeemer, frees what is hidden in the innermost soul of men. That is accomplished by embracing the vitality provided by Mythos.

MORTAL FOR EVERYONE, YET NOT TOUCHED BY THE CYCLE OF EONS.

Mythos of the Stone innately demands redemption. The word redeem is utilized primarily in a mythological sense in that freedom relates to wholeness of the individual personality. It is the participation in a process honoring the "forbidden thing's" role in freeing one from attachments by activating the creativity of change. It facilitates the flow of energy from the innermost reaches of the soul into the activities of life. According to Joseph Campbell the sin of missing the mark is a stagnation found in "the waste land of an inauthentic life."

Jung adds: "In civilized man the rationalism of consciousness, otherwise so useful for him, proves to be the most formidable obstacle to the frictionless transformation of energy. Reason always seeking to avoid what to it is unbearable antimony, takes its stand exclusively on one side or the other, and convulsively seeks to hold fast to the values it has chosen. It thereby excludes any symbolic view of itself. Without this awareness, too many gaps remain unfilled in the man's experience of life and each gap is an opportunity for futile rationalizations. False causalities will be preferred to truth every time."[13]

Who are the potential candidates for submission to an active role in a redeeming drama, savoring the mysterious dimensions of transformative fruition? The answer may come from intellectual curiosity or "something else." To bite and savor the forbidden fruit, allowing one to become intoxicated with the ripened images originating from a sacred, archetypal tree "an apple a day keeping the doctor at bay."

Matter of Timing — Receptivity

*The questions posed by the guardians
of the Way to the Stone*

Are you in the midst of a recent chaos, involuntary submission, and have yet to discover a capacity to respond creatively? When conflict has exhausted your resources and you feel impotent, are you without a "home"? You come to doubt yourself. Your previous system of beliefs and previous way of coping with life have been threatened or shattered. Abandonment, exposure and danger occur at such moments; an agonizing event from which there seems to be no way out, guided by dictates of the conscious mind, and cultural thinking.

Are you curious about a creative meaning beyond therapeutic management? Is it possible to consider that within the "punishment" there is a blessing? Apocalypse and Illumination have a shared definition and revelation, bringing to light or uncovering a source of renewal. The treasured stone, previously hidden is revealed.

Have you reached a stage of life where the traditional or popular concepts and values do not provide an effective transitional bridging? Specifically, at midlife and beyond, when the logos serving you well during earlier stages of life now feels inadequate? The modern dilemma presented by the magnitude of an aging population confronts us with a challenging array of impossible tasks, whose healing requires heroic deeds in order to experience the transforming vitality of archetypal images.

Are you curious about the analytic psychology of Carl Jung? Then you are attracted to his forum as a means of further exploration. Within his analytical format mythological tales and their imagery revel in the drama of dreams and life, actively revealing unknown aspects of the individual psyche essential for the goal of individuation.

Is the belief and faith in the defining cultural paradigm or spiritual dogma, outer authority, serving you effectively? Are your emotional needs or the sense of security dependent on the acceptance and support of that defining "outer authority"? If so, then do not allow the precious stone, individual experience of your uniqueness to "poison your well."

The complete wisdom of the Trickster is present when the meaning of mythos is actively embraced. This perception reveals a mystery whereby the conflicting and disintegrating experiences of suffering have the potential for implementing something new into life. This paradox is a process originating from the regulating center within, the unconscious archetype of wholeness.

The scenario of the forbidden thing and the role of the archetypal trickster is a universal timeless combination. Such as the well known tribulations initiated by the forbidden actions of Eve, Judas, Pandora, Psyche, Percival, etc. The well known Greek myth has Pandora removing the lid of a great vessel releasing a swarm of sorrows allowing the earth to become full of evil.[14] It was the "forbidden" deed which placed her in a sorority with Eve and Psyche.

Moses Challenge

To manifest archetypal healing, the "mystery," it must be allowed to express itself on its own terms without prejudice. It is called the Moses challenge.

The following is from the Koran; Sutra 18;

Khidr appears as the spiritual teacher or director of Moses in the Koran. The name of Khidr meant the "Green One," indicating his wisdom was always fresh and eternally renewable, archetypal. Moses is the mortal one who seeks, the man on a quest begging for instruction, but it is Khidr, the Trickster, who tells him that he will not be able to understand.

Moses said to him: "Shall I follow you so that you may teach of the good you have been taught?"

He said: "You will not be able to bear with me. And how will you bear with what you have no knowledge of?"

Moses said: "You will find me, Allah willing, patient and I will not disobey any order of yours."

He said: "You follow me, do not ask about anything, until I make mention of it."

So, they set out; but no sooner had they boarded the ship than he made a hole in it. Moses said "Have you made a hole in it so as to drown its passengers? You have done a grievous thing."

He said:" Do not reproach me for what I have forgotten, and overburden me with hardship."

Then they departed; but when they met a boy, he killed him. Moses said: "Have you killed an innocent person who has not killed another? You have surely committed a terrible deed."

He said: "Did I not tell you that you will not be able to bear with me."

Moses said: "If I ask you about anything after this, do not keep company with me."

So, they went on, until they reached the inhabitants of a city. Where upon they ask its inhabitants for food, but they refused them hospitality. Then, they found in it a wall about to fall down, and so he straightened it. Moses said:" Had you wished, you could have been paid for that," Khidr said:" This where we part company. Now I will tell you the interpretation of that which you could not bear patiently with."

"As for the ship, it belonged to some poor fellows who worked upon the sea. I wanted to damage it, because, on their trail, there was a king, who was seizing every ship by force. As for the boy, his parents were believers; so we feared that he might overwhelm them with oppression and unbelief. So we wanted that their Lord might replace him with someone better in purity and closer to mercy. And as for the wall, it belonged to two orphan boys in the town; and beneath there was a treasure for both of them. Their father was a righteous man; so your Lord wanted them to come of age and dig up the treasure, as a mercy from your Lord. What I did was not of my own free will. This is the interpretation you could not bear with patiently.

"In the beginner's mind there are many possibilities, but in the expert's there are few. The mind of the beginner is empty, free of the habits of an expert, ready to accept, to doubt and open up to all possibilities. It is the kind of mind which can see things as they are which step by step and in a flash can realize the original nature of things. It is to experience them without need to control them."[1]

Jung adds, "If I am to understand an individual human being, I must lay aside all scientific knowledge of the average man and discard all theories. I can only approach the task of understanding with a free and open mind."[16]

It is difficult to accept the "Moses challenge." We discriminating mortals are taught to interpret behavior or objects of experience with the ethical criteria of good and evil, right or wrong, by mundane or worldly rules of engagement. When the containing or dominate thesis, "good," is threatened by an antithesis, "evil," we tend to fanatically condemn and reject the value of its opposing or alternative premise, those cultural creeds which have evolved over time. Therefore, allowing the Self to manifest on its own terms is a task for the personality who deviates from the norm.

Without synthesis, unconscious projection has the opposites locked into a fanatical and irreversible alienation with apocalyptic consequences. Thus we become possessed, embraced by fear and its accompanying violence. The current worldwide tensions dramatically reflect that scenario.

Therefore, the definition of wholeness now includes accepting the value of destructive happenings or recognizing forbidden things that were previously repressed or positive values not accepted. The dynamism of the Stone strives to integrate them into your conscious experience, the life you live. Find a positive value in those circumstances and you will honor those people who have hurt you as necessary tricksters.

By illuminating and exposing "gods" and "animals" from their secret recesses you release a potential surge of enthusiasm, living a more versatile life. The consequences of suffering become modified, evolved. Otherwise you must unwittingly and literally bear the reciprocal burden of scurrilous physical and emotional consequences. Jung said that we see nothing in the human psyche that is more destructive than unrealized, unconscious creative impulses.

Everyone loves a conspiracy theory. Energetically the grandiose state, collective thinking, as logos spirit of the rock fears and therefore, as consciousness seeks control or domination over the material body and events of life. But, for each of you receptive souls, the jurist, this Elder seeks to illuminate your verdict.

My introduction of the Way of the Orphan Stone encourages your acceptance of the conviction that physical and emotional aspects of life also contain a mythos version of secret messages from a mystery seeking equal expression in the "court of the suffering." The mythos declaration opposes "medication without equal representation."

Apocalyptic Dream

The following dream metaphorically reveals the dual nature of the trickster archetype, apocalyptic and redemptive: I am an individual who lives in a coastal area serving in the community as a physician. There is concern about the possibility of an impending doom. One individual man who is the leader in the community has given the prediction for the event, but not the timing.

Suddenly it is here and at that moment everything in the city is destroyed or vanishes. Structures are devastated by some invisible force that is not atomic, biological, or chemical. I wondered what to do and I realized that anything not destroyed had been looted and carried away in ships. It happened so quickly and efficiently that the one responsible for the plundering must have planned it in advance. No one steps forward to take charge in the chaos.

In searching for that someone I discover a hidden treasury in an abandoned building. In a devastated place there is an open vault containing golden bars giving me a feeling of joyful enthusiasm. Preparing to depart with the gold I meet a small young man who is clothed in the garb of a monk, his face seems familiar. His ambience presents a sense of simplicity and humility by the nature of his clothing and the quality of his voice. He invites me to have a cup of tea with him, which I curiously accept. The mysterious fellow then brings forth an ancient copper teapot and pours two cups of tea.

As we sit sipping the tea the mystical host points to an empty space in a nearby building and tells me that its emptiness presents the opportunity to create a new way of life that does not exclude the holy (redemptive healing).

I reflected upon the symbolism of this transformational dream: It was situated in a coastal setting symbolically suggesting it is near the unconscious. The authority (Self) pronounces that a way of life is doomed, involuntary submission without options. This drama symbolizes as an initial invisible destructive phase of an archetypal Trickster at play. It is the equivalent of discovering that you have an incurable life threatening disease or painful, irretrievable loss. The solidarity of the logical ideals that define your life expectations faces an involuntary disruption.

When adaptive projections fall away, a loss, the ego is typically in chaos, suffering, which stimulates the search for a savior (hero) who provides a diagnosis with external remedies. The traditional doctor-patient relationship is thus constellated.

There is no outer savior in this dream. Instead it presents the image of gold which in alchemical terms is the transformed personality or attitude. The Self then comes forth as a youthful image of a humble monk representing the redemptive aspect of the trickster and announces the wisdom of filling the empty space of something missing with that which does not exclude the holy (redemptive healing).

Ritual Elder

The redemptive process of the Stone is an individual experience, but is rarely accomplished alone. This statement contains a critical stipulation that on the surface seems to be a contradiction. Therefore, as an archetypal pattern of initiation, it necessitates a ritual elder as defined by Robert Moore in his book, "The Archetype of Initiation, Sacred Space and Personal Transformation."

The Ritual Elder as facilitator is an outer guide with the duty of protecting the boundaries of transformational space thereby avoiding a misadventure. In addition, it is the one who patiently facilitates the disciplines of amplification and reflection thereby welcoming the symbolic messages emanating from the evolving soul while in the sacred space. It is a companion who appreciates the disciplines of the Sacred Dance, therefore does not reject them, but instead actively dances with them.

The Ritual Elder assures the sacred space is not invaded by disrupting forces and achieves fruition which means the transformed personality then returns to mundane space, avoiding a chronic entrapment in sacred space; one who is astute enough to intuit, is wise enough to make their guiding statement, or to ask a question in service to the Mystery of the Stone.

It is essential that he or she has the capacity for mythic reflection which does not sacrifice the mystery of the individual soul upon the altar of common allegory or category dictated by traditional thinking. The Way of the Orphan Stone is robbed of its unique characteristics when subjected to the leveling experience of logical evaluation or subjected to ethical parameters. Religious and philosophical institutions grant validity to experiences only insofar as they conform to their ideological standards. The entrance into the halls of their "truth" is forbidden for the "fools of mythos."

I look forward to understanding whatever the Trickster in all of its personifications makes available to me, but I also concede that there are dangers associated with those initiations. Jung warns us that development of the personality is one of the "most costly of all things." For me Kyle's death was the ultimate test of Jung's proclamation.

Opening up to the archetypal realm of experience is a crucial event in the evolution of my personality. And, I understand that the process of the Stone does not serve to palliate my adversity, but it involves me in a dynamic activity which manifests values and meanings of an archetypal nature beyond my burden of personal suffering. The candid nature of those revelations demands a sacrifice of innocence which is a price very few are willing to pay.

The archetypal dynamism of the Trickster challenges the function of any creed and/or belief system, secular religion you are yoked or paired with. Those ideological sanctuaries which attract your devotion and ultimately shape the nature of your interface are the challenges imposed by the Trickster. Whither cometh the tricks and what defining response does the Way of the Stone offer? The participating orphan finds a redeeming answer as the trickster mysteriously transforms into the "Yoke-ster."

LEVEL THREE

WALKING THE WAY

Heaven above
Heaven below

Stars above
Stars Below

All that is above
Also is below

Grasp this
And rejoice

— Kircher, "Oedipus Aegypticas" p. 414

CHAPTER 7

YOKING

Introduction

I will put my best foot forward by wrapping words around the ambiguous mystery of yoking as it relates to the Way of the Stone. For this orphan a metaphoric hybridization is accomplished and a logos offspring produced, by conceptually yoking psychology and mysticism. True to the Stone, a few will be served by the potential wisdom this errant child has to share, because its message risks being condemned as foolish fantasy-heresy. More ideally, in the spirit of yoking, its message would be both foolishness and wisdom.

Confronting the Trickster's redeeming role in the death of Kyle means dealing with my own centre. This is the essence of yoking; to reconcile suffering with wholeness; to become the wise old fool.

For the sake of discussion I divide the nature of yoking into three possibilities, although in experience they do not always exist in such distinctly separate categories.

The Mundane

It is a secular or exoteric word. It denotes a subjective experience relating to or typical of this world, and conforms to the creeds of collective dogmatism which risks being alien to the divine nature of the individual soul. It is a state whereby one is yoked primarily to worldly values. Every "spiritual truth" turns into something material, becoming no more than a tool to achieve happiness or gratify the secular "needs" of the faithful. Thereby the idea of God is caught up in human attributes.

Typically the orphan "fortuitously" occupies a safe home exclusively dependent upon the modern science of facts and/or faith in the literal theology of a specific religion or a secular-philosophic cause. The meaning of experience is dependent upon concrete parameters and understanding is essentially dependent upon faith in the subscribing context. In this field of a material reality, symbols become allegories to escape the ambivalence of symbols.

Creeds of dogmatism: every formulation that achieves official status becomes snared in orthodoxy and literalism and the concept of either statistical "normality" or pathology. "Anecdotal" is a heretical word. It is a disturbing idea for those logical minds who would steal from the individual a key ingredient of creative change. In addition the obsession with causality produces false contexts as it attempts to find healing where it is not present. As a consequence, the culture is witness to an escalating dependence upon drugs and alcohol. In other words every member of a culture struggles to survive its "diseases" and "weaknesses."

Traditional mundane prayer is an offer of thanksgiving or petition for something, i.e., to remove feelings of fear or gratify the desires of intent. It represents a will to power or achieving conditional happiness. Those who are obsessively yoked with the mundane seek to make their daily lives stable, predictable and happy, and made rock solid by attachment to the literal sentient mundane values. As a consequence mundane values are ceremoniously imposed upon the domain of religious prayers.

The grandiose consciousness, threatened by the Trickster's chaos is driven to manipulate images for achieving some spiritual wish, a search for a medical cure, a favor toward personal betterment, enhancement of happiness by calming fears or desires, or stimulating some other magical counteraction. All these desires of the ego are sought at the risk of suffering an inner poverty.

In a four millennium process the grandiose human ego has created a mundane God in its own image. Each religion steadfastly attempts to defend or evangelistically impose its concept of God on everyone and believes its creed is the absolute and only path to salvation.

Metaphorically each religion claims its brand of detergent is the only effective one. If an individual does not accept this belief as the only truth and fails to use it as directed he or she risks leaving this life in a "dirty" condition. This rigid belief of exclusion creates orphans, lost sheep, who in innocence do not realize that the dark side of love might be the need for power.

"Logically, the opposite of love is hate. Where love reigns, there is no will to power; and where the will to power is paramount, love is lacking."[1]

In addition, modern technology labors to compensate. It attempts to make this lack of compassion, or one-sided containment, tolerable by providing salvation through providing psychotherapeutic pharmaceuticals and/or "spiritual" beverages.

Consequently the individual can be led to believe that he or she is adequately served by the dictates of mundane reason and authority and the absoluteness of causality. It has excluded recognition of and respect for the individual as a mystical entity. Therefore, the direct experience of the Divine and the mystery of the Stone is excluded because it is not entertained as having a useful or primary function in the achievement of well being.

"It is only in the modern societies of the West that non religious man has developed fully. In other words, he accepts no model for humanity outside the human condition as it can be seen in the various historical situations. Man makes himself, and he makes himself completely in proportion as he desacralizes himself and the world. The sacred is the prime obstacle to his freedom. He will become himself when he has become totally demysticized. He will not be totally free until he has killed the last god. He recognizes himself in proportion as he frees and purifies himself from the "superstitions" of his ancestors."[2]

It is impossible to completely dissolve the Stone-soul of the individual into one-sided collective ideals, but it is never totally identical with it. When the integrity of the Stone is completely absorbed by the logos of traditional societies there is dis-ease. The orphan by definition is a unique archetype that cannot be totally identified with anything else, understood, or rationally explained. It cannot be altered by some act of will nor contained within some orthodox creed which restricts truth to some closely held values it has chosen.

Proclamations from Orphans

Ralph Waldo Emerson

"As Men's Prayers are disease of the will, so are their Creeds a Disease of the Intellect."

There is the collective exception: the orphan's diseases of prayer and intellect may serve as a healing elixir for all others until the Trickster intervenes.

Albert Einstein

In the same regard, "For me they are nothing more than the expression and product of human weaknesses and wishful thinking."

In the Way of the Orphan Stone their creeds represent a mundane prison, but for the vast majority of "lost souls" those creeds and their petitioning prayers offer a haven of salvation and source of security which serve until the Trickster says otherwise.

The above paradox as summarized by Jung: "It is really the individual's task to differentiate himself from all others and stand on his own feet. All collective identities, such as membership in organizations, support the "isms," and so on, interfere with fulfillment of this task. Such collective identities are crutches for the lame, shields for the timid, beds for the lazy, nurseries for the irresponsible; they are equally shelters for the poor and weak, a home port for the shipwrecked, the bosom of a family for orphans, a land of promise for disillusioned vagrants and weary pilgrims, a herd and safe fold for lost sheep, and mother providing nourishment and growth."[3]

Today, modern economic and scientific accomplishments have taken over as the key paradigms for solving problems and defining successes.

Thereby, an emphasis is placed on outer resources for healing and resolving problems. Consequently, an affinity for the transcendence of Eastern spirituality is flourishing as a compensatory means of finding a sufficiently inverted attitude with which to work out problems from within, instead from without.

Transcendent

Twenty years ago in what now seems like some faraway place, I encountered the seemingly impossible task of meditation. For one year I struggled to have any experience. Transcendental Meditation came to my rescue. Through senior guidance and use of my mantra it happened. After a few months of practice I realized Nirvana was not a nurturing home for my orphan personality.

From the transformational view point Jung says:

"People will do anything, no matter how absurd, in order to avoid facing their own souls. They will practice Indian yoga and all its exercises, observe a strict regimen of diet, learn theosophy by heart, or mechanically repeat mystic texts from all over the world—all because they cannot get on with themselves and have not the slightest faith that anything useful could come out of their own souls."[4]

Siddhartha by Herman Hesse

This treasured book tells the story of an orphan journey in Buddhist terms. He begins his quest with complete submission to the ascetic way of life.

"Siddhartha had one single goal—to become empty of thirst, desire, dreams, pleasure and sorrow—to let the self (mundane ego) die. No longer to be self, to experience the peace of an emptied heart, to experience pure thought—that was his goal. When all the self was conquered and dead, when all passions and desires are silent, then at last must awaken, the inner most of Being that is no longer self—the great secret."[5]

After the initial ascetic experience he ventured into the mundane world of pleasurable experiences. He lived the worldly life as a prosperous merchant with gusto which also included fathering a son. The disruptive trickster eventually brought that second phase to an end. It was a chaotic experience which initiated him into the third stage of his quest, a river boat ferryman. Then like the Stone, he yokes two sides of the river called life metaphorically serving the symbolic function of Hermetic consciousness.

"It corresponds to active imagination, in the matter of a bridge joining two banks of a river. The crossing itself is essentially a hermeneutics of symbols, a method of understanding which transmutes sensory data and rational concepts into symbols and making them effect this crossing"[6]

At the ending of the book Siddhartha is talking to his friend Govinda at the river's edge. He bent down, lifted a stone from the ground and held it in his hand and said to Govinda, "This stone is a stone; it is also animal, God and Buddha. I see value and meaning in each of its fine markings and cavities. I love it, because it has long been everything and always is everything."[7]

Stone

Charles Schulz, *Peanuts* cartoon

Lucy talking to Linus: You can't drift along forever. You have to direct your thinking—for instance you have to decide whether you are going to be liberal or conservative. You have to take some type of stand—you have to associate yourself with some sort of cause.

Linus responds: Are there any openings in the lunatic fringe?

There is a significant way to participate in the lunatic modes of reflections activated by the Stone. It is different from the more traditional prayer containing human aspirations and petitioning the divine for favors. It is not a request for something or a meditative experience of mindless transcendence. It is a reflective mode of being that seeks compassionate union of human consciousness with one's divine presence. This yoking activates one's creative imagination and the dynamism of one's symbolic reflection.

Materialism and transcendence are logical opposites. They are hostile brothers, two different methods of grappling with the powerful influences from the unconscious each compensating for and/or denying its existence.

The Stone's rendition of true introspection sees that mundane materialism and divine presence are no longer adversaries, but yoked as complementary partners. In psychology it is called reconciliation of opposites and when complemented with candid honesty has the affect of candescence. The redeeming nature of the trickster is revealed through the light of wisdom.

"Two implies opposition. Two is the separation of one thing from another and represents a state of conflict. Three, however, is the sum of one and two and unites both within itself. It is the reconciling symbol that resolves the conflict state of two."[8]

Eros of the Stone, as the third, yokes the two, transcendent and mundane, whereby suffering is altered, because it is understood and experienced in relationship to an inner mystery. This yoked relationship liberates a creative force by being cast astray from the conceptual schemes imposed by guardians of traditional creeds.

As a consequence our "diseases" and "weaknesses" of the will and of the intellect become less bothersome, and require less compensating medication and behavioral adjustments. This is because the events that occupy them never limit themselves to simple social or material parameters of mundane experience. Instead they always express or symbolize some inner happening.

The archetypal mystery is such a complex and ambivalent source of wisdom that a simple logical expression never does it justice. Therefore the individual works with unique symbolic images as they arise, not ones chosen by a code or master. Psychologically this means the Self comes to realization on its own terms rather than on terms of the ego (The Moses challenge).

The images that the Trickster provides are sources of meaning whose "reality" rests upon the unique personal testimony of the Stone. The experience of suffering is therefore interpreted as an irrational call for change in rational "management." A feeling of enthusiasm is experienced by activating the energy of an inner authority from which cometh the tricks (Wills suffering).

From Zen Buddhism we learn about the attachment of non-attachment. Not to be attached to any society is to be aware of its collective value, but at the same instant, non-attached. Embracing the Stone is standing alone in one's own truth. Each of us is individually and collectively yoked. Therefore, our well being depends upon the collaboration of both. It is not being exclusively bound to one at the expense of the other.

To achieve a more creative healing scenario, the disciplines of the solitary one declares that there is the intimate individual experience of yoking two aspects; mundane "I" and transcendent "I." It is a dual activity within the individual soul. One is far from excluding the other but rather is interpreted through the other. The unifying "I" is at the centre while the "I" of the conscious personality dances in an attentive circle around it.

You might appropriately ask: "Who am I" as this paired identity? For the sake of wholeness the answer is not limited to the mundane activities of life or escape into the transcendent, but also includes the symbolic, mythos, dimensions of experience. Those hidden treasures relate to us through images provided by individual dreams, myths and various art forms. The human soul is no longer something separated from the eternal mystery by logos. Absolute bondage to outer realities championed by traditional religious beliefs and scientific materialism all fall aside.

Two Concepts for Yoking

Psychologically: "At all events, the aim and effect of the solemn round dance is to impress upon the mind the image of the circle and the centre

Vishnu mandala, Nepal, 1420
This is an example of the basic archetypal configuration of the Mandala.

and the relationship of each point on the periphery to that of the centre. Psychologically this arrangement is equivalent to the mandala and thus is a symbol of the Self. The Self is not an ego, but a supra-ordinate totality embracing the conscious and the unconscious."[9]

Mystically: "It is this quest that represents the circumambulations around the temple of the "heart"; that is around the mystery of the Divine Essence. But the visionary is no longer the solitary self, reduced to his mere earthly dimension in the face of the inaccessible Godhead, for encountering the being in whom the Godhead is his companion he knows that he himself is the secret of the Godhead, and that it is their "syzygia," their two-ness which accompanies the circular processional."[10]

When I became 58 years of age the dominance of the mundane world with its material, social accomplishments met an apocalypse made of big time Trickster stuff. As a consequence of that initiation an incarnation of the friar sense of reality progressively introduced a second way of interpreting experience. That transformation of my personality was facilitated by being initiated into the imaginative realms of the mystical heart that subsequently introduced me to yoking experience of mythos with logos. Within this space I came to know the existence of an imaginative presence. The seeds were sown which flowered into the Way of the Stone.

Heart as Centre

The heart, when functioning as a mystical state of being, is beyond and different from contemplation. It stimulates imaginative activity which serves as a transformative process rather being solely defined as a "mindful experience" of transcendence. I approach meditation much like a vision quest or a divination with a question at times when I am emotionally uneasy. I ask "what ails me?" On other occasions I seek a deeper knowing and a joining in harmony with the particular event at hand.

"The heart is considered the organ that produces true knowledge, comprehensive intuition and gnosis by the mystics of all times and persuasions. It functions as an intermediary between the world of mystery and the sensible world. It produces symbolic images which are perceived by our imaginative function. In contrast the rational theologians prefer to use the idea of allegory."[11] (Thereby escaping the ambivalent nature of symbols.)

From the Old Testament, "the tradition the heart symbolized the inner personality and its emotional life and was the seat of wisdom and understanding. The heart was to the internal personality what the body was to the external. For every ten times the word heart is used in the Old Testament for the bodily organ, there will be a thousand instances of its employment in a metaphoric sense."[12]

At your point in life have you as an individual had a meditative experience and have you been initiated into a spiritual process? In the *Caduceus* book I tell of the initial difficulty I encountered and its resolution by joining a meditation group and using a mantra. This opened the door for my later initiation into heart centering. Centering as contemplative meditation has received acceptance by ecumenical religious groups and is one source for induction into an altered state, but the heart as centre is different.

The Practice

I begin my submission and induction into the heart center by sitting in a position which is physically comfortable. My hands are positioned on my mid chest over the physical heart, called the fourth chakra, placing one hand on the top of the other, thumb tips lightly touching. Next I close my eyes and bring my focus upon the breathing with a gradual sense of increasing relaxation. Feeling some degree of calmness, I turn my focus exclusively to the hands upon the heart. They seem to be one. Various sensations may occur, but the most frequent are a warmth or tingling vibration. It is then that I chant silently the attributes of the heart center: compassion, innate harmony, healing presence, and unconditional love synchronous with my breathing.[13]

Once in a dreamlike altered state I await the manifestation of symbolic images and/or messages gifted to me by my brother from mythos, the Friar. He represents a mythological motif whereby helpers spontaneously appear and/or synchronistic phenomenon happen which guide me, the errant orphan.

As images come forth as active or passive imagination there is a yoking of the outer "I" with the inner "I." The attributes of the heart center all occupy the core of this meditation and state of being. When consciousness is united with its related archetypal images it is transformed into peace in the midst of chaos. This experience of innate harmony or objective feeling free from affect is encountering experience beyond subjectivity.

In this sacred space of innate harmony one feels a healing presence and images not dependent on desire for outer remedies or divine intervention. The endless search for happiness dependent upon external gratification shifts to a state of joyful participation in life. This state is created by blending the mystery of archetypal creativity with the mundane experiences of the visible, sensory world.

The sacred communion between the peripheral "I" and its centre is the pathway to Stone-Hermetic-Christ consciousness. This gives rise to the realization that instead of being immersed in rational arguments based on cause and effect, it transforms the Giver into the given; the hidden treasure "yearning to be known."

It is the knowing of one's self with a sacred knowledge that is capable of giving a transcendent dimension to the mundane state of being human. It is a gratification of an individual's yearning for knowledge of both divine and human nature or quality. It is my outer personality, turning inward, which invites simplicity, heart-inspired feelings, art of imagination, and capacity for symbolic reflection, entering the expansive archetypal worlds of depth psychology and mysticism.

If we fail to yoke this twofold dimension of the visible and invisible simultaneously we lose the innate integrity for the Stone and its capacity for symbol cognition. This common essence is not through evidence derived from cause and effect. It is the experience of compassion, a reciprocal and simultaneous attraction, between the individual and his or her inner healing presence. In other words, there is a constant reciprocity between the divine yearning to be human and human yearning for experience of the divine.

From the Orphan Stone inscription:

I HAVE TO BE FETCHED OUT OF THE DEEP LIKE A
FISH OR FALL LIKE A WHITE STONE FROM THE
HEAVEN.

Christians, as well as many alchemists, believe the importance of Christ consciousness is given by the fish symbol. Hermetic philosophers and alchemists also connected to the Stone for the same reason. For them it similarly illuminated and deepened the meaning of Christ. History reveals that disciples of the rock chose the Fish as their allegory. Hermetic and Gnostic advocates are more inclined to favor the Stone as their symbol.

My continuing quest for the Stone as a means to effectively enact this yoking process brought forth the realm of sacred dance, specifically of the Round Dance. The Round Dance, performed by Christ and the twelve disciples is the metaphor chosen to illuminate the process. This activity enters a process of circumambulation with the twelve aspects of one process, the progressive movement toward unity with one's Centre. In this particular example it symbolizes developing Christ consciousness.

As a process, the Hymn initiates (mystical Hermetic) Stone consciousness, the intermediate realm of experience between human (ego) and divine (Self). This synthesis of outer consciousness with the "divine authority" within the individual as an archetypal pattern is not limited specifically to Christ consciousness. However, for our purpose of illumination it serves well as an effective metaphor.

"The Mystical Round Dance which Christ instituted before his Crucifixion. He told his disciples to hold hands and form a ring, while he himself stood in the centre. As they moved round in the circle, Christ sang a song of praise."[14]

Christ as a symbol represents the central source of life energy, the unifying center within. If you are non-Christian you may prefer to use an alternative adjective, i.e., mystic, hermetic or stone, instead of Christ. All mystic disciplines, regardless of title, symbolically serve the craft of the Trickster. They forever challenge the integrity of a fabric woven by reductive literal thinking, the creeds favored by the modern mind set.

"A vacancy in the human heart: man felt the absence of the "inner Christ" who belonged to every man, Christ's spirituality was too high and man's naturalness too low. The images initiated by Trickster—Stone glorify itself in its own way; it could transform itself into spirit, but on the contrary, fixed the spirit in stone. The Stone may therefore be understood as a symbol of the inner Christ in man (Sophia's Wisdom). The divinity of Christ has nothing to do with man but the healing Stone is extracted from man, and every man is it potential carrier and creator."[15]

The treasured experience of the divine Christ is more than mere attention to the historical Jesus. It is a state whereby the scriptures are interpreted symbolically and the meaning of Christ is acquired through an inner experience.

Jesus said "I will pray the Father, and he will give you another Counselor (Paraclete), to be with you forever, even the spirit of truth, whom the world cannot receive because it neither sees him nor knows him; you know him for he dwells with you, and will be in you." John 14:16. The Paraclete, as described in John, can only be seen as an individual inner guide who supersedes Jesus in history and dogma. It is the "inner Christ" of Meister Eckhart or in psychological terms, the Way of individuation."[16] (In mystical terms it is the Way of the Stone.)

By metaphorically singing with the sacred, we prepare for a renewal and redemptive value in which the personality is transformed, especially suffering. This is because the thinking "mind" and the feeling "heart" dance to the same rhythm. It is equivalent to the state that Buddhism defines as "being in the Tao" or the Christian's designate as a "state of Grace."

"Are we to understand the "imitation of Christ" in the sense that we must copy his life and, if I may use the expression, ape his stigmata; or in a deeper sense that we are to live our own proper lives as truly as he lived his individual uniqueness. It is not an easy matter to live a life that is modeled on Christ's, but it is *unspeakably harder to live one's own life*, as truly as Christ lived his."[17]

My hidden and primary function, introverted feeling, which Kyle and I shared became consciously active. "Its aim is to not adjust itself to the object, but to subordinate it in an unconscious effort to realize the underlying images. It is continually seeking an image which has no existence in reality, but strives after inner intensity, for which the objects serve at most as a stimulus. Fundamental ideas then possess a value beyond those selectively imposed solely by intellectual concepts."[18]

I humorously designated my own aberrant condition as the "Opus Psychosis," "A place in the lunatic fringe." It is a malady one shares with poets and heretics thus being free to dance with ghostly apparitions. Being the weird one among the sane and righteous I found I had to face the risk of mocking and exile by the austere guardians of tradition. Even so, true to the alternate reality of the Stone, I am privileged to discover domains inhabited by archetypal images. From this mystical space come answers which challenge the sanity of logical meanings.

"When you relate to your own (transcendental centre), you initiate a process of conscious development which leads to oneness and wholeness. You no longer see yourself as an isolated point on the periphery, but one in the centre. Only subjective consciousness is isolated; when it relates to its centre it is integrated into wholeness. Whoever sings the hymn and dances the dance sees oneself in the reflecting centre and his or her suffering which the one in the centre "wills to suffer."[19]

The process of gaining this wisdom of the Stone is commonly met with a great deal of resistance because attachment to subjective suffering is master of the moment. For me Christ's Hymn of the round dance creates an objective state of being which harmoniously yokes my psychological process to a divine presence, thus the cloud that obscures healing insights begins to dissipate. The Stone question, "what ails me," becomes an invitation to heart center. At other times I enter the process of yoking by activating its disciplines while singing the Hymn of the Round Dance.

As previously stated, the Wisdom of the Stone given to this grieving father is simply one way amongst the vast accumulated strategies recorded during humankind's historic struggle to survive omnipresent adversity and suffering. Certainly there are "different strokes for different folks."

Say not, "I have found the truth," but
Rather "I have found a truth."
Say not, "I have found the path of the soul."
Say rather, "I have met the soul walking
Upon my path,
For the soul walks upon all paths."

— Gibran, Kahlil, The Prophet, p. 54

CHAPTER 8

CHRIST'S HYMN

The Round Dance

The Mystical Round Dance was instituted by Christ before his Crucifixion, but was cast astray by those who initially established church doctrine. It is an integrative synthesis of outer consciousness yoked with the dancer's inner "divine authority." Much like Jung's orphan stone the editors of the New Testament deemed it a misfit and cast it astray. One may find reference to the Mystical Round Dance in the Apocryphal St. John.

When performing the dance myself I was astounded at its mystical effect upon my process. Afterwards, contemplating its exciting effect, my entire yoking process evolved. Tears came to my eyes when the feeling of candescence filled my body and soul. It seemed to make all those years of study, heart meditations, and numerous initiations worth every moment I devoted to them.

"Christ spoke to his disciples instructing them to hold hands and form a ring while he himself stood in the centre. As they moved around in a circle, He sang the hymn of praise.

> Grace paces the round, I will blow the pipe,
> Dance the round all, Amen.
> The twelve paces the round aloft, Amen.
> To each and all it is given to dance, Amen.
> Who would not the dance mistakes the event, Amen.

I will be saved and I will save, Amen.
I will be freed and I will free, Amen
I will be wounded and I will wound, Amen

I will be begotten and I will beget, Amen.
I will eat and I will be eaten, Amen.
I will be thought, being wholly spirit, Amen
I will be washed and I will wash, Amen.
I will be united and I will unite, Amen

A lamp am I to you that perceive me, Amen.
A mirror am I to you that know me, Amen.
A door am I to you that knock on me, Amen.
A way am I to you the wayfarer.

Now as you respond to my dancing, behold yourself in me who speaks....

As you dance ponder what I do, for yours is this human suffering which I will you to suffer for you would be powerless to understand your suffering had I not been sent to you as the logos by the Father.

If you understood suffering, you would have non-suffering. Learn to suffer, and you shall understand how to not suffer... understand the Word of Wisdom in me."[1]

The Heresy

To be astray from accepted thought and rational understanding, breaking free from a static state of being, is perceived as heresy and often interpreted as being dysfunctional. The conventional paradigm is a grandiose collective method that attempts to protect us from adversity, but it also deprives us of individual experience, the profound mystery.

This situation creates a fundamental problem. The nature of suffering by an individual cannot be logically determined. It is fraught with contradictions; it is irrational. In addition we are conditioned to believe that the outer sense of personality (ego) is the center of one's universe and must assume full accountability for its suffering and failures. Suffering is also related to the Self, the one who stands within one's centre. With the round dance I feel a union of two aspects of suffering bringing me into a fellowship with archetypal images and yoking me with their messages of healing.

The Way of the Orphan Stone finds itself in the infamous company of heretics, or Astray Orphans. It is characterized by an archetypal form of personality, and it challenges conventional wisdom. Nicolaus Copernicus of the sixteenth century A.D. proposed the heliocentric model which placed the sun as the center of our universe rather than earth. This was an overt contradiction for the dominating theological doctrine of that time. He evoked silence to prevent punishment. This proved to be prudent since Galileo spent the last part of his life under house arrest and Giordano Bruno was burned at the stake by the church for insisting upon the same thesis.

The process of yoking proposes that the ego (earth) is not the center of the soul, but rather the Self (sun). Life unfolds by their alchemical interaction in a dualistic cauldron of symmetry. It is apparent that the inflated collective psychology does not hold a similar view. It will not voluntarily relinquish its concept of being the center of its universe. As a contemporary example, some idealists take the stance that humans are totally responsible for global warming while disregarding the greater contribution provided by the interrelated cycles of both sun and earth.

The Trickster has frequently surfaced in my life. The dictates given to me by ego bound disciples failed. It is then that the candescence way of the Stone yokes my suffering with creative meanings beyond those previously taught to me by traditional logic.

A yoking is not possible as long as the ego thinks it is the centre, and that everything in the psyche is of its own making, denying archetypal influences. My experience of the Way of the Stone brings with it the realization that I am not actually the master of my own house. Nor was Kyle in his fates and destiny. I came to eventually realize that there is an autonomous inner director separate from the ego called the Self. When antagonized it brings about suffering. "When the inner man wants something different than the outer man we are at war with ourselves."

Instead of a pathological diagnosis yoked upon me by the trickster to be exclusively palliated by the modalities of modern medicine or psychological coping, it is a call for introspection. The Way of the Stone became my call to an introspective process or journey. The process of the yoking dance accelerated the process of become more conscious and candescent.

The Process

I realized the consciousness communication between the outer sense of "I" and the archetypal psyche is an awakening; a transforming healing effect upon my personality. But how is this healing accomplished? Up to this point, the theoretical wrapping around with words had fed the appetite of the intellect, but had lost its validity for this mythos activity of the soul until it became ontologically practical.

You might ask, "what is the essence of this yoking experience?" By creating a heliocentric shift to the centre of your universe as the Self (sun) with the ego (earth) you have created an intermediate third level of candescence, or Stone consciousness. This experience necessitates attention and devotion to the twelve disciplines which actively engage this mystery.

Water takes on the color of its container, or in other words the attitude of the observer. Therefore, I must admit that my many years of exposure to Jung's analytical psychology colored my engagement with the Hymn of Christ's round dance. I identified with the process which Jung called individuation. In my individual experience it became a hermetic or Stone process.

Ralph Waldo Emerson.

"Every man's condition is a solution in hieroglyphic to those inquiries he would put. He acts it in life, before he apprehends it as truth."

Regardless of the context in which it is explained. the process of the dance serves to accelerate the transformation of the personality. It changes the meaning of suffering by altering the effect. I find it possible to achieve a certain transpersonal, archetypal value, by accepting the centre of my universe as the inner "I" (sun) rather than the outer "I" (earth) and their synthesis, which is the yoking experience of the Christ consciousness.

The Sacred Hymn is a compassionate process that fosters an intimate interaction, a yoking, between the personal outer "I" and the divine centre of each participating individual, the inner "I," initiating the Stone-Christ-Hermetic Consciousness. As a metaphor, the hymn and dance result in the movement or activation of archetypal energy. It is a hidden inner force that becomes active in feeling and tone. The Dance is a celebration of candescence while suffering is celebrated in darkness in the valley of the shadow; the wasteland. It all depends upon the nature of one's conscious relationship with the Trickster.

Technology's success can only be achieved if it devotes attention to scientific rules of engagement. This is a logos activity. The challenging activities of your life, the outer world of conscious activity, negative or positive, constitutes the prime source of meaning.

Likewise, the practical application of symbolic apperceptions can only lead to success if they are practiced with the same discipline and devotion. This mythos experience is a creative force that produces your dreams and fantasies. It is vital for the aspirant to have adequate knowledge of the methods and discipline essential to initiate yoking, and maintain the interface with the dynamism of archetypal ideas.

There is a certain state of mind that becomes activated by the process of the yoking in which suffering is transformed into wholeness. It is achieved by the Hermetic process based on the Sacred Hymn. As previously quoted from Jung, "it is a matter of being devoted, of being conscious of everything one does and keeping it constantly before one's eyes in all its dubious aspects—truly a task that demands a great deal." (Attention and awareness)

What are those specific activities which create the mythos experience and guide a specific character or personality striving to submit? Which specific activities communicate with and activate a certain wisdom given by an "inner authority"? It is necessary to define the words I use in order to see how they fit the metaphorical aspect of the yoking process. A devotion to the Way of the Orphan Stone requires certain disciplines defined as the:

"Training expected to produce a specific character or pattern of behavior; especially experience that produces moral or mental changes.[1]

While cultural morality is a set of ideas about what is right, there is an absolute reality that guides the seeker and produces candescence. Perfect honesty or candidness with oneself is a moral key which is essential for unlocking the transformational process of the Round Dance.

A Disciple of the original hymn and dance was "One who embraces and assists in the teachings of another." (3) In service to the definition the disciples of the rock served as church apostles, vouched for the historical Jesus, and testified for the necessity of faith in orthodox creeds as provided by church authority, thereby establishing moral codes.

In contrast, the sacred Hymn of begetting has twelve functions or attitudinal states of being. As an inner movement it yokes with the "inner authority" and facilitates the experience of Christ-Hermetic-Stone consciousness.

Migne, P.L.

"For what does it avail us if we are to investigate carefully and understand rightly the nature of things, yet do not understand ourselves."

92

The Twelve Disciplines

"The spirit of truth, whom the world shall not perceive because it neither sees Him nor knows Him, for He dwells in you and will be in you." John 14:17

1. I will be saved and I will save, Amen

The Discipline of Individual Experience

"One pearl of great price for which a man went and sold all that he had, and bought it. It was the well guarded secret of the individual."[1]

The stone as a jewel is called a solitaire. By implication it defines the errant orphan as opposed to a devoted member of some organized group.

Christ says: "Blessed are the solitary and the elect, for you will find the Kingdom! Because you were issued from it, you will return to it again. Many stand outside the door, but it is only the solitaries who will enter into the bridal chamber."[2]

Psychology also tells us, "Every advance always begins with the individual, conscious of his isolation, cutting a new path through un-trodden territory. To do this he must first return to the fundamental facts of his own being, irrespective of all authority and tradition and allow himself to become aware of his own distinctiveness."[3]

In contrast, the statistical analysis derived for a collective sense of value obliterates everything unique. It seeks to yoke experience and meaning to mundane values in order for the dynamism of the orphan to exist,

"It is important to live life with the experience and therefore the knowledge of its mystery and your own mystery. This gives life a new radiance, a new harmony, a new splendor. The big question is whether you are going to say a hearty yes to your adventure."[4]

The empirical, grandiose "I" essentially excludes the hidden knowledge of the archetypal psyche. Its intellect, by the action of its inherent imperialism, imposes orthodox criteria and value and for the sake of cultural uniformity as a vehicle for common education.

"It is higher than the fulfillment of collective ideals, which are all nothing but make shifts and conditions for bare existence. Collective ideals are not by a long way the breath of life which man needs to live. If his soul does not live nothing can save him from stultification. His life is the soil in which his soul can and must develop. He has only the mystery of his living soul to set against the overwhelming might and brutality of collective convictions."[5]

Entering the Way of the Orphan Stone as a grieving father I actively surrender to a process of introspection. (What ails me?) I place my suffering on the altar of a more profound mystery instead of strictly yoking my state of grief to mundane or orthodox counseling. Thereby I am allowing archetypal epiphanies to potentially heal me.

> "Be vigilant, and allow no one to mislead you by saying:
> Here it is! There it is!
> For it is within you.
> — *The Gospel of Mary Magdalene.* 8: 15–19

This quote represents the central essence of the orphan. It is an individual experience rather than a sole act of faith. It is an idea that has excommunicated, or torched at the stake numerous Christian mystics during the earlier history of the Church, and whose authority as an intermediary of salvation must be protected at all costs. The shadow side of truth implies that the desired end justifies any scurrilous means.

Paraphrasing my favorite tale from Zen Buddhism, the ox herder searched everywhere for his lost ox. During a prolonged quest for the missing ox he encountered many proclamations on how and where to find his lost ox, but all failed to reveal its location. Then one day in a candescent instant he realized he was the ox.

While on the way, guided by the Stone, I experienced that the direct apperception of the invisible rests upon my unique personal testimony. This is in contrast to being limited by strict adherence to the conceptual schemes expressed by logos.

Where "anecdotal" is a heretical word, the pursuit of my wholeness reflects my unique personality and must be considered the key ingredient for creative change in my life. This way of interpreting experience is in contradiction to the conditional paradigm where the nature of my suffering is only valid when completely based upon the empathetic dictates of traditional mentality.

Through mystical eyes there is a hidden existence of an intermediate world between observed objects and the unknowable, peripheral consciousness and archetypal determinates. This assumption is a paradox. In these modern times when our happiness is largely bound to the pursuit of physical perfection and intellectual supremacy over matter, space and time, we tend to ignore the underlying mystery of life.

Mary Magdalene — The Orphan

Andrew began to speak and said to his brothers, "Tell me, what do you think of these things she has been telling us? As for me I do not believe that the Teacher would speak like this. These ideas are too different from those we have known."

Peter added, "How is it possible that the Teacher talked of the matters with a woman, about secrets of which we ourselves are ignorant? Must we change our customs and listen to this woman? Did he really choose her and prefer her to us." *Gospel of Mary Magdalene,* 17:9-20

The popular book authored by Dan Brown, *The Da Vinci Code,* concretized the essence of the Mary Magdalene Gospel by suggesting she conceived a child with Jesus thereby establishing a physical blood line. In my view it is "conceivable" that her "womb," as chalice, was impregnated with Christ Consciousness, the mystical blood line for Christianity. With this mystical "going astray" being the Stone, the unacceptable orphan, the "church" must aggressively keep it a secret.

"This is a great secret which can be revealed by God himself. Here is found the stone which the king wears in his crown, Wise women hide it, foolish virgins show it in public, because they wish to be plundered. Popes, certain priests and monks revile it, because it was so commanded of them by God's law."[6]

History has informed us that the heretical, mystical version of the Passion of Christ stimulated spectacular acts of overt suppression. The torture and executions justified by the established Church was exclusively devoted to the Rock which was given the name of "Peter" by Jesus. The foundation of rock, alias logos, upon which Roman Catholicism was established along with the acceptance of the cross as an allegory for the suffering of Jesus. Meanwhile the deeper symbolic mystery was lost.

"The definition of the cross or centre, the boundary of all things, is exceedingly original, for it suggests that the limits of the universe are not to be found in the nonexistent periphery, but in its centre. There alone lies the possibility of transcending this world. The cross symbolizes order as opposed to the disorderly chaos of formless multitude. Its centre being totality and finality contains everything and therefore is free of opposites."[7]

Thereby, in the earthly field of opposites, the authority was established by Roman Catholicism and later Protestantism. Constantine initiated the summons to establish the official creed for the Roman Catholic Church. The editing council of Nicaea (325 A.D.) canonized the Synoptic Gospels and Letters of the New Testament as the absolute authority for Church dogma. The Roman intellectual community and their will to ecclesiastical *power* experienced a field day.

Simultaneously they excluded all "heretical" Gnostic gospels (at least thirty) as the stones gone astray. Among these orphans was the *Gospel of Mary Magdalene* who represents the "womb" or Holy Grail of the Stone. It is the mystical, Hermetic consciousness whereby personal experience trumps ideological faith.

Mary Magdalene says, "Lord I see you now in this vision." The Lord answered, "You are blessed, for the sight of me does not disturb you.
—*Gospel of Mary Magdalene*, 10: 12-15

I see the church's rejection of Mary Magdalene as a vain attempt at resolving a serious breach in religious conformity, but her Gospel wholeheartedly reinforces my own quest for understanding the Way of the Stone.

2. I will be freed and I will free, Amen

The Discipline of Submission

To set free is a function of redemption which begins with an act of submission. This is a discipline which necessitates the sacrifice of outer attachments, while refraining from deifying or demonizing the persons or objects of experience. Making the statement, "I will be freed and I will free," signifies one who is freed from the persistent distress of personal entanglements and allows submission and access to one's own archetypal mystery, the centre, or "the one who wills to suffer." This represents a use of the term "freedom" in the mythical sense of redemption from causality rather than the secular act of paying a debt or the religious salvation from sin.[1]

Achieving that wholeness we call healing is not a simple task someone does for you, singularly or collectively. It is the most difficult of challenges since its accomplishment may demand that you "sacrifice attachment" to what you have cherished most, the forbidden task of the individual experience.

Every successful transformational initiation benefits your personality, but on balance also demands the sacrifice of a universal, archetypal pattern. Few people volunteer to go there, but all troubled souls blindly struggle with it. "Suffering happens."

The reflective Way of the Stone gives one a clear experience of the healing process which follows the stillness of an introspective dance. In the absence of thought the light of candescence fills a "darkened" soul with images of wisdom. Consciousness gains one more advocate.

I said to my soul, be still, and wait without hope
For hope would be hope for the wrong thing; wait without love
For love would be love for the wrong thing; there is yet faith
But the faith and the love and the hope are all in the waiting
Wait without thought, for you are not ready for thought:
So the darkness shall be the light and the stillness the dance.

— T.S. Eliot

I say, "So the dance shall be the prayer and suffering the light."

Thus, sacrifice of your desires and submission into your sacred trans-formational centre opens the portal to objective reality. It is not letting one's self become irreversibly paralyzed by the never ceasing relativity of purely subjective experiences. Jung defines this affectivity, neurosis, as a state of feeling characterized by marked physical response on the one hand and a peculiar disturbance of the ideation process on the other. To consciously sacrifice this chronic attachment to subjectivity and its affects is "forbidden" by modern thinking. In many cases patients find that the forbidden task is an impossible challenge and gratefully avoid, palliate or cure with the aid of medication or coping techniques, the choice being logical instead of mystical.

"It is a true sacrifice (act of submission) only if I give up the inten-tion of receiving something in return. The offering would inevitably have the character of a magical act of propitiation, with the purpose and tacit expectation of purchasing the good will of the Deity. That proposition is ethically worthless.

"Consequently the gift always carries with it a personal intention, for mere giving of it is not a sacrifice. It only becomes a sacrifice if I give up the intention of receiving something in return. If it is a true sacrifice, the gift must be given as if it were destroyed. There grows the most costly task of sacrificing oneself or at any rate that part of myself which is identical with the gift."[2]

I place my personal involuntary sacrifice of grief upon the altar of mythos without expectations. The Trickster that came and took the dearest part of myself, my beloved son, is forgiven for its participation in the process. My hymn of disciplines continues as the dance becomes my prayer, my suffering the light.

In the Old Testament there is a story that best illustrates the same process of forgiveness as my act of redemption. Joseph's brothers abandoned him as a young boy. As a consequence he was taken into Egyptian slavery. There, by interpreting prophetic dreams, he gained favor with the Pharaoh. He subsequently ascended to authority in the Egyptian court. Many years later he met the brothers who had betrayed him. They feared his retribution for what they had done to him, but it turned out differently.

From the Old Testament we read: "Then Joseph said to his brothers, "Come closer to me." When they came closer to him he said, "I am your brother whom you sold into Egypt, but now do not grieve, do not reproach yourselves for having sold me here, since God sent me ahead to preserve your lives. God sent me before you to assure the survival of your race on earth and to save your lives by a great deliverance. So it was not you who sent me here but God." [3]

Thus, an act of suffering is in the eye of the seeker. The prayer of the dance changes the nature of the cauldron of suffering just as Joseph changed the nature of guilt.

Joseph thus set himself and his brothers free. No pardon or retribution was required. The redemptive value of the Trickster was honored. This scenario represents the basic meaning of forgiveness. There is nothing to forgive. True forgiveness is the state where you no longer see yourself as an isolated victim stuck at some point on the periphery. You see yourself as the One in the centre of your circle of experience in direct contact with the divine presence.

Yet without the compassion of a mystical experience, harmful circumstances might well defy my capacity to forgive. Therefore, the manifestation and function of the transforming trickster does not always miraculously heal, and often is perceived exclusively as an agent of tragic wounding. True forgiveness happens when I give positive value to the one who apparently hurts me. My reaction to a mortal wound ultimately demonstrates the nature my relationship with the trickster.

In other words, on an impersonal level, Joseph felt free because there was nothing to forgive. That is the ultimate sign of forgiveness; freedom. Yet on a personal level you may experience events so horrific that they defy your capacity for forgiveness. Your staunch faith in "goodness" makes it impossible to accept that the God you worship in heaven would do such a thing. Therefore, as a human I find religiosity telling me that it must be a consequence of my doing caused by some other person, or must be the work of Satan.

The discipline of freedom is in accord with the necessity of the trickster's fateful wounding. Suffering is required to initiate or guide us along the path of our destinies. This realization frees us. In contrast, the gift of pardoning offenses may soothe the conscience, but only offers a conditional forgiveness.

True to the mythology of the trickster, something, some condition, is always required in return for wisdom. First, redemption and freedom from the original wounding is conditioned upon my realization that my suffering has a transformative purpose! Secondly, I must free my soul from captivity, the temptation to become the victim. My true forgiveness of the trickster only happens when I shed the cloak of the grieving victim, and embrace the wisdom that Kyle's life and death served as an archetypal destiny.

The following experience is a dream I had relating to the discipline of submission. I am in a small stone enclosure. Looking about I realized that I lay on an altar-like marble table. In that same moment fear grips me when I become aware of a huge male lion pacing around where I lay. Frantically looking about, I see no way to escape. Defenseless, I anticipate a brutal death. The lion approaches the altar and begins sniffing my body, starting at my feet. His hot breath on my skin gives me a cold sweat of fear. He progresses slowly upward toward my neck and head. I expected at any moment to feel myself gripped in his jaws and ripped into bloody pieces.

Realizing no course of action during this disparate situation I resign my fear, relax, and submit to my anticipated gory fate. At that instant of peaceful acceptance I sense warm, wet licks across my chest and heart. At that numinous moment I am possessed by serenity and break out in joyful laughing, realizing that instead of the bite of death I am receiving licks of love. My submission, thus experienced, is an act of courage rather the pathological shock of the victim's fate.

Dream images have powerful messages for me. You may wonder how this relates to the activity within my own unconscious psyche. At the time of the dream I was facing the unpleasant prospect of submitting to bilateral knee surgery. In reflection I asked myself, "Will my act of submission transform my fearful encounter with the Trickster?" Will it empower me to set aside my fear of surgery and receive a redeeming "lick of love" from the Trickster?

3. I will be wounded and I will wound, Amen

The Discipline of suffering as a Call for Renewal

Joseph Campbell gives us insight into the nature of suffering, "Myths tell us how to confront and bear and interpret suffering, but they do not say that in life there can or should be no suffering. But, you don't mean compassion condones suffering, of course compassion condones suffering in that it recognizes that suffering is life." (Buddhism)[1]

This discipline declares that every step in the Orphan Stone way is necessary to advance the wholeness of personality, and can be accomplished only at the cost of suffering. When worn as a badge of honor, wounding plus healing equals wholeness. When worn as an affect of the victim state, wounding without healing equals chronic disease. The challenging distress is not a punishment or a moral issue. It is an indispensable means of leading one to where life intends to take him or her. The trickster is thereby given a positive value.

Seeing myself as the Orphan of the Stone I only seem to learn from my tragic times. Like a bright neon light the question flashes, "Who am

I that all this should happen to me? What ails me?" I am not asking what is wrong with me. To find the answer to my fateful question I must look within my own soul for the origin of suffering. In other words, I find out my subjective experience of suffering is the prime material for the work of redemption. Jung used the term "prima materia" for the task of undergoing alchemical transformation. After the initial wounding and emotional reactivity, the inward activity of stone consciousness is activated.

I was freed by the ritual of communion. I escaped the emotional entrapment imposed by outer causality. I joined in the dance with mythos and saw myself in the reflecting centre and knew that my suffering is what the One who stands in the centre "wills to suffer." The examination of my grief reminded me that Kyle and I are objects as well as subjects, not always the master within our own houses or hopeless victims of the "so-called" unfortunate events related to his death. Instead, it is my realization of the archetypal dynamism within the experience that I receive a redemption gift from the trickster.

Repeating Words from "The Redeemed"

"The way is not without danger. Everything good is costly, and development of the personality is one of the most costly of all things. It is a matter of saying yea to oneself, of taking oneself as the most serious of tasks, of being conscious of everything one does and keeping it constantly before one's eyes in all its dubious aspects—truly a task that taxes us to the utmost."

Suffering is a plea for introversion, entering your inner garden in quest for your soul. As previous stated this is extremely difficult for those who must interpret experience exclusively with an extraverted attitude serving causality. The intellectual mind denies the genuine nature of suffering. Reductive thinking seeks to explain it rationally, as the consequence of something secondary, denying the validity of the underlying archetypal dynamics. Conscious introversion is a process that always leads to a candescent outcome, even that it may end in death.

Suffering is the key to the underlying dynamics which results in redemption. Jung reinforces that concept: "So we see nothing in the human psyche is more destructive than unrealized, unconscious creative impulses."

When outer palliation is less than effective, or a cure is determined to be medically impossible chronic suffering ensues. It is then conceivable to acknowledge the voice of the trickster and thus discover previously unknown inner resources of which one has no prior knowledge. In the spirit of completeness one should allow equal opportunity for the trickster's contribution to our capacity to survive and thrive through the experiences presented by the fateful challenges of life.

All twelve disciplines presented are pertinent to illuminating the question, "what ails me?" Again, this is not the question "what is wrong with me"? Rather it is a question of redemption through suffering. The introduction of this initial triad of individual experience, active submission and creative suffering, sets the stage and prepares me for the subsequent disciplines of the hymn and dance which engages my grief as a transformational process.

Intellectually, it is possible that every outer effect must conjure up or manufacture an outer causality. Otherwise, it has no logical reason to exist. In contrast, it is conceivable that perceived effects and causes represent paradoxical aspects of a single phenomenon; one with a basis for existence, one without.

With a release from the shackles of a binary association, the one that can be recognized as being with outer causality then becomes free to engage a greater mystery with the hymn and dance for deeper meaning. I have found that you cannot trick the trickster. But…you can yoke with your center to acquire a deeper meaning. It is this experience of innate harmony which invites a healing presence.

My intent for choosing to travel the Way of the Orphan Stone is to "know" those attributes of wholeness. It is to reap love, not material fruits or personal power. It is a love for the candescent process regardless of the outcome. Fame and fortune have been pleasurable companions during certain periods of my life, but for the orphan they have proven to be fickle lovers. In the end "something was always missing."

As an individual who submits his grieving to this process, and examines the mythos nature of suffering I have been plagued with questions. Several of those questions took priority as I bring my grief to a dance with the disciplines of the hymn.

What were the details of the drama surrounding Kyle's life at the time of his death?

What was the nature of our relationship?

Is my grief complicated by any feelings of guilt?

How have I functioned as a trickster in his life?

What things have changed in my personal and professional life since I have had the experience?

What can I do or not do as a result of this unwelcome event being imposed upon this stage of my life?

What effect does his way of life and the manner of his death impose on the family and friends who loved him? Is there a specific message for his old father?

Did I have a dream, fantasize, or see visions prior to or during the process? This is to identify mysterious images which offer archetypal guidance.

What was the nature of the language I used to describe the drama? Etymology of words can reveal symbolic messages. The images and patterns manifesting from the archetypal mystery have codes of communication which include the archaic origins of words. Do my symptoms of grief also represent symbols pointing to a deeper mystery beyond my personal sense of loss?

Did Kyle or I sacrifice aspirations earlier in life for adaptation, or to gratify alternative considerations? A denied innate archetypal aspect of my personality, wholeness, may now be calling for my attention, a healing modification of my contemporary identity.

What wisdom might I gain by metaphorically reflecting on Kyle's life and death?

In his early teens Kyle became fascinated with books about mystical adventures and one particular mystic image. He was especially enchanted with a black panther he called Tasselhof. As a replica, the above statue was given to him as a Christmas gift during those magical times of his life.

I will attempt to answer as many of those questions as I can from a mystical-archetypal point of view in the subsequent disciplines. Thus, the activity of begetting is initiated.

4. I will be begotten and I will beget, Amen

The Discipline of Listening

There are two modes to the discipline of listening. The first mode requires listening empathetically in the search for clues to those signs that lead to a means for palliation, or cure, within established concepts. Medicine cabinets today are filled with sophisticated but costly medications that squelch the voice of the Stone. Bookshelves overflow with popular manuscripts whose words of advice for the pursuit of happiness stifle or impair the apperception of symbolic meaning. In plainer words, the dictates of logic and emotion prevail over an orientation process. **Outer mechanistic ideas dominate**. It is the search for causality that is demanded by medical science that devise means to empathetically palliate causally defined effects. When our illness is informed by professional diagnosis, we are driven by an innate need to make it go away. The voice of the stone is squelched by the collective's persistent desire to counteract suffering. It fails to ask the Stone question, "What ails me"? This is the way of the rock.

A second mode requires that the facilitator compassionately listen to the story of the illness which often reveals its soulful intent; it's hidden ontological, creative purpose. In this mode **inner messengers dominate**. The illness is allowed to symbolically speak to us, thus activating the language of images. This infuses the vitality of compassion, and opens the psyche to the opportunity of initiating the process of redemption.

Begetting is thus the art of unconditional listening, and being aware that inner messengers and outer mechanistic ideas may coexist in the same experience. Those who practice this way of begetting become one world with hermetic wisdom. It is a conscious relationship in rhythm and rhyme with the soul's yearning to be heard—an inner quality of hermetic compassion. To enter into resonance with the moment is an attentive activity that demands a specific quality of presence and truly listening. The Way of the Stone of begetting is having audition that attentively hears the "still small voice from within"; a yearning to be begotten.

"Those who are meant to understand will hear, those who are not meant to understand will not hear."[1]

So, begetting is archetypal listening. It is a basic and essential skill for the individual to adopt an attitude for seeking out the symbolism of what is heard. Where there is no conscious relationship to the inner processes, it is difficult, though not impossible, to receive the messages underlying the subjective reactivity of outer consciousness.

The words of logos used by the paradigm of science serve as the exchangeable coin in intellectual commerce. However, the same words gain life and meaning when I also apperceive their symbolic meaning in relationship to my grief. I know that archetypal mysteries are not to be solved but I can develop an active relationship with them through the language of symbols. Apperception is a psychical process of apprehension of symbolic language. The understanding of symbolic apprehension makes Stone listening possible. Apperception is related to mythos; to close the eyes and mouth. "In the stillness is the dancing."

This aspect of the transformative process "hears" the voice of the Stone. It attunes to the mysterious inner voice espousing an incentive for transformation, serving the process of "begetting." The initial impetus for meandering on this path into my inner nature is at the centre of suffering. Suffering energizes reflection, and reflection energizes the intent of "getting inward," to find my imagining soul.

Then, I enter a symbolic, but real quest for "getting it." An essential maturation process takes place. It may stimulate the Stone query, "what ails me?" I must face the consternation of "getting it outward." The reward of asking the essential question stimulates a renewed "It." Mythic consciousness brings to my human nature the transformed personality which participates more harmoniously in life. This is the true reward for suffering. In respect to finding the divine aspect of one's Self it is the Holy Grail.

The Way of the Stone is a process that entails not only listening and engaging with a detached consciousness, but also playing with my moods and associated symbolic images, giving them form and expression. I journal the symbolic messages as they are revealed to me by inner authority. Dreams and various forms of artistic expression are the essential prime materials for later reflection, introspection, and amplification.

Supplementing logical knowledge with the Way of Stone wisdom is a path to the candescence of consciousness emanating from a mythos alternative. It gives me a more wholesome picture of my human experience. Begetting is beautiful. It is a conscious act of communion.

5. *I will eat and I will be eaten, Amen*

The Art of Communion

In spite of the reader's limited understanding of my mysterious candescence, I must share the orphan secret. It serves by benefitting my psychic well being. Its hidden content no longer can work as a poison alienating me from communion with a few other folks. It keeps me from being kidnapped and isolated by unrelenting fantasy.

This discipline introduces two levels of communion; the realm of personal secrets found in the outer "I" and the contrasting domain of the archetypal mystery, found in the inner "I." To explain the contrast, a secret can be fully known intellectually, but the archetypal mystery is only partially interpreted through the experience of candescence.

The personal secret is a projection of one's shadow; an aspect projected upon another and disowned or repressed by the ego. To get to the personal shadow and implement healing the conflict must be confronted. It is the sacrifice of innocent purity which implies the realization of the shadow. It identifies one with the role of an innocent victim, and the tendency to project the activity of the trickster onto Satan, his enemies, neighbors, or family members.

Jung says, "If a projected conflict is to be healed, it must be returned to the psyche of the individual, where it had its beginnings. He must celebrate the Last Supper with himself and eat his own flesh and drink his own blood, which means that he must recognize and accept the other in himself. For if you have to endure yourself how will you be able to rend to others also?"[1]

If I am going to honest with myself concerning my son's death and do justice to it, I must confront my own shadow and my relationship to his own secret, the black mask. My conscious repression of that reality for the sake of a cherished persona, blocks my Way to the Stone. It weaves a web of deceit which will entrap and sicken my soul.

"To cherish secrets and hold back emotions is a psychic misdemeanor for which nature finally visits us with sickness—that is, when we do these things in private."[2]

This is my challenge: to make the ritualistic process of the black mask conscious, and to achieve a relative honesty about my relationship to my son's closely guarded secret. Otherwise, the grieving for his death will plague me indefinitely. It is an unconscious presence radiating toxic emissions that relentlessly poison my physical and emotional well being.

Although hiding its content serves my perceived need for cultural acceptance, it continues to torment me unconsciously. My grieving leaves my soul unhealed. As long as I fail to accept ownership it is not integrated, and it will unconsciously torment me.

"The psychological rule says that when an inner situation is not made conscious, it happens outside, as fate. That is to say, when the individual remains divided and does not become conscious of his inner opposite, the world must perforce act out the conflict and be torn into opposing halves."[3]

At the gateway to my personal secrets the creative process of my transformation of grief met the guardian against redemption called guilt. An archetypal, protective, humbling agent present when one is not ready for initiation. I succumbed initially to this encounter with shame by announcing that Kyle's sudden death was due to a ruptured brain aneurism. I feared traditional morality and the judgmental stigma of sin and guilt related to his ritual of the mask. I temporarily wandered off the candescent Way of the Orphan Stone by violating the rule of absolute honesty.

"Kissing the wound" is a metaphor. It confronts the trickster face to face. This dynamism is exemplified by a tale about St. Frances of Assisi. He possessed a powerful aversion to lepers, finding them nauseating and repulsive. He absolutely avoided them until one day a leper with open decaying wounds abruptly appeared on his path. Initially he wanted to retreat, but instead an impulse to kiss the wounds overwhelmed him. It was the most unthinkable and repulsive act imaginable. Facing his inner repulsiveness, and kissing the wound it symbolized transformed him. Simultaneously he was no longer repulsed by the wounds of the lepers.

"Although of great inner value, the "prima material" is vile in outer appearance and therefore despised, rejected and thrown on the dung heap. Psychologically, this means that the "prima material" is found in the shadow, a part of the personality that is considered the most despicable. Those aspects of our selves most painful and most humiliating are the ones to be brought forward and worked on."[4]

As a mortal human it is not possible to experience a life devoid of aversions or fears. We fall to their mercy and tend to become victims. Then we repress or project our wounds. Yet in service to the Stone they carry the potential to vitally inspire us with their many emotionally laden meanings. Mythology, as a carrier of meaning, universally presents us with a wealth of tales about those transformations achieved by intimate contact; i.e., kissing the frog or encounters with the dragon. My personal secret about the cause of Kyle's death was my wound to be kissed.

This redemptive process opens my understanding to **The Archetypal Mystery**. Facing my grief and the process of Kyle's death motivated my own intent to explore a deeper meaning for his life and death. It prompted me to explore the world of mythos for understanding, an opening to the creative mystery beyond the entanglement of secrets. It involved a communion with the creative mythology of masks.

"In the Last Supper a synthesis takes form of participation in the body and blood of Christ, i.e., there is ingestion and assimilation of the Lord and in the round dance there is a circumambulation around the Lord as a central point. Despite the outward difference of the symbols, they have a common meaning: Christ is taken into the midst of the disciples"[5]

According to Jung, the maximum degree of consciousness is achieved when the ego is confronted with its projected shadow as exemplified by a personal secret. It is also a contemplative experience of archetypal consciousness which has its own specific contents that emerge from unknown depths. They become available to me for conscious illumination of my own personal drama through the mystical celebration of the Last Supper.

Jung says, "A symptom can be transformed into a symbol through awareness of its archetypal foundations. Every symptom derives from the image of some archetypal situation. For instance, many anxiety symptoms have as their archetypal context the hero's fight with the dragon, or perhaps the rites of initiation. Many symptoms of frustration or resentment are a re-enactment of Job's archetypal encounter with God. To be able to recognize the archetype, to see the symbolic image behind the symptom, immediately transforms the experience. It may be just as painful, but now it has meaning."[6] To get rid of the symptom may deprive one of an opportunity to realize a candescent moment.

My challenge was to identify the archetypal basis of my son's death, my own grief, and suffering. I realized that an understanding of the bridge between emotion, suffering, and candescence is essential to the process of becoming conscious. I further realized that the same process is possibly the essential purpose of life itself.

In the study of near death experiences, one of the essential and common explanations includes an encounter with a being of light who asks the question, "What is in your heart and what have you learned? This can be interpreted as, "In what way have you become conscious?" This is life.

"If the image is charged with numinosity, that is, with psychic energy, then it becomes dynamic and will produce consequences. It is a great mistake in practice to treat an archetype as if it were a mere name, word, or concept (allegory). It is far more then that; it is a piece of life, an image connected to with the living individual by the bridge of emotion."[7]

Symbols refer to a mystery. This aspect is essentially lost when elaborated by the dictates of institutional creeds. In those settings, for effective communication and teaching, the symbol becomes an allegory or a code. Communion with my archetypal source, the Hymn of the Round Dance, takes me back to the priority of individual experience, the Way of the Orphan Stone. It gives me a sense of my process in relationship to the archetypal mystery.

As a mystery I discovered that my connection to candescence is lost in translation by proclaiming it a personal secret to be solved or kept, rather than candidly shared. The mystery of the archetypal dimension, independent of signs and codes, is neither an intellectual puzzle to be solved, nor a doctrine, or a moral issue to be judged. Thus, to the distress of the logical "needs to know" of rational literal minds, some aspect always persists in hiding as a mystery beyond the "secret."

True to the transitory nature of a visitation into Sacred Space, one is blessed by the fall into a "reality" inhabited by archetypal images and impersonal awareness. Isolation by the personal experience of the archetypal mystery is, with difficuulty, a blessing communicable to only a few and perhaps impossible for all others. The benefit is yoking the subjective nature of ordinary reality with the objectivity of non-ordinary reality. It is truly coming to consciousness without going ontologically astray.

Traditional literal theology portrays the trickster aspects of the mystery as a demonic figure. A mythos identity points to the presence of a central archetypal trickster content which exacts a tribute of constant regard and attention from peripheral consciousness. Thus, we suffer.

The Trickster in this aspect innately serves to activate and infuse an energetic response for the maturation of my conscious personality. This manifestation challenges my subjective psyche. The inherent negative and positive interpretations comprise two aspects, personal and universal archetypal images, contributing to my own wholeness. These images are vital to creating my personal reality. They establish a relationship with the divine aspects of one's self, as well as a compassionate relationship with all living beings—even rocks and stones.

In other words, thought images are a holy communion between the world of senses and the act of leading a mystical life in which there might be a conscious stream of messages, and to which we assign the archetypal name, "The Messenger" to explain the relationship.

6. I will be thought, being wholly spirit, Amen

This is a certain Discipline of Images as Messengers that relate to one's journey on the Way of the Orphan Stone.

"Images are not what we see, but a way of seeing." Edgar Casey

In current usage, the term "imaginary" is equated with the unreal; with something that is outside the framework of being and existing. It is a modern rendition that denies the authenticity of the world of mythos. Henry Corbin in "Mundus Imaginalis" points out that there is an intermediate reality that is well served by the imaginative function. (1) Without the imagination it is impossible to have ideas. Yet the common impression is that something not perceived by the senses or derived from facts is unreal and imaginary.

"The impression exists because the usual and customary perception of images refers to a concrete reality, those which subjectively influence the ego. For the question of meaning: the outer event by itself can never create meaning, but is largely dependent for this on the literal interpretation given to it by the observer, referred to as "concretizing" of the symbol. There is more to reality than what meets the "discerning eye. The concrete event by itself can never create meaning, because it is largely dependent on the manner in which it is understood."[2]

The mythic use of image is not a perception experienced by the senses or faculties of the physical organism, but rather an intermediate power which has a creative role. When recognized symbolically, the primordial image remains alive because of its feeling value. What is involved is the psychical organ that makes possible a transmutation of inner states into outer states, and into sensory-events symbolizing the inner states. The images that heal us emanating from our depths are not restricted by the information available to our senses.

"One experiences the image making power of the unconscious in context with understanding the archetypal dimension of the psyche. He is given access to a broader, ego transcending wisdom. This means that it is connected to a trans-conscious reality which is beyond the categories of space and time. This corresponds to the phenomenon described by Jung as synchronicity. Such experiences are likely to occur when the archetypal level of the psyche has been activated and they have numinous impact on the observer."[3]

My life has been enhanced by ever increasing experience of this phenomenon. The following instance occurred while functioning in the persona of a doctor of alternative medicine. A 50-year-old retired combat Marine had retired from active service two years previously. During the difficult transition between serving as a warrior and becoming a peaceful citizen, he began to experience chest pain upon physical exertion which prompted him to seek the services of a cardiologist. After a "work-up" a major coronary artery obstruction was revealed whereby the cardiologist immediately planned to schedule bypass surgery.

The marine would have no part of it, and adamantly refused to submit with the steadfast assertion that excess iron in his body was the "real" problem. The cardiologists vehemently rejected his untrue assertion as fantasy based on their evaluation and scientific expertise. There was no medical basis in fact. He then sought an alternate appraisal which brought him to my office. Listening to his wild fantasy intrigued me, but as a physician I also felt medically inclined to disprove its reality.

He presented as a stocky muscular male with a body tattooed by multiple scars from extensive battle wounds. The other physical findings, including the blood pressure, were unremarkable. Blood tests that included measurements for iron levels were also within normal limits, except moderately elevated serum cholesterol. There was no rational basis for his fanatical idea of excess iron in medical terms.

I had listened to this ex-marine as a physician seeking a logical or scientific basis for his fantasy. In pondering the follow-up consultation, I felt an inner uneasiness. This called for a shift to my friar mode of listening. Instantly I was hit by a candescent, synchronistic revelation.

Seated before me was the archetype of a battle-scarred Mars, the warrior of Roman Mythology. His fantasy now had its reality. Symbolically, iron is the metallic designation for this mythological personality. The Mars warrior survives by the strength of steel, which is the aggressive nature required for engaging an enemy in war. He possessed a personality which was not compatible with a peaceful transition to a citizen. A compensatory outlet at this time such as competitive sports was contraindicated based on his diagnosis of coronary artery disease.

He was innately seeking a ritual of transition. I accommodated him by giving his "fantasy" its due. I advised regularly donating blood to the blood bank, thus removing iron from his body. This procedure actually and symbolically decreased the psychic potency of the warrior archetype.

He was given the following creative visualization, a play with images. Once he was comfortably situated in the phlebotomy recliner he was to begin the ritual by centering on his breathing to promote further relaxation. When ready he visualized the iron flowing from his body as he was releasing the essence of his warrior blood. That essence was saved in another container for transfusion into those who needed his warrior steel in the struggle for survival.

The phlebotomies were his rite of passage serving his transition to a peaceful citizen. His non-scientific fantasy being iron ladened was thus gratified. My deed done, he returned to the cardiologist for follow-up care. This individual possessed a powerful warrior complex which initially demanded resolution on the level of mythos rather than logos. A fortunate synchronistic revelation came to his rescue.

"Any patient is treated correctly when he is treated as an individual. This means not giving him an explanation based on scientific principles that goes completely over his head. The first duty is to keep close to the living facts of the psyche, to observe the facts carefully and thus be open to a deeper experience."[4]

During my process of begetting as in a personal transition, images arose spontaneously. Images have their fate. They may be utilized as signs to delineate a prescribed course of action or they may also be perceived as the best possible way to represent meanings difficult for the logical mind to grasp. Symbolical amplification applied to specific images arising during periods of struggle or duress can bring to candescence metaphorical insights revealing the mystery of begetting. The change demanded by creativity and symbolized by the Orphan Stone are stimulated by the candescence brought about by the Round Dance

Through the symbolic function of images we see the hidden existence of an intermediate world between observed objects and the unknowable. Thus, I discovered the Orphan Stone or Christ consciousness. The images manifesting from the unconscious are given the same intrinsic mythic value as sensory perception. A "hidden treasure is revealed," and candescence is achieved. The lost treasure is found.

Once the mythic value was recognized, images betoken of something that is illusionary became real and meaningful. They are messengers whose stealth is detected by a mind tuned to creative symbolism. The inner images may originate from either the personal unconscious as insight or the archetypal mystery as demonstrated in dreams.

"Because there are images there is symbolic cognition."

7. I will wash and I will be washed, Amen

The Discipline of a Symbolic Life

The way of the Orphan Stone is a life that actively participates in the recognition of symbolic truth. Without symbols there would be no Way of the Stone. It is essential to accept that every human psyche has unconscious contents and every observable object has an unknowable side. A symbol serves the Way of the Stone by yoking the two halves of a token, thereby establishing a logos connection to the mythos half of experience, the missing part of "knowing" why we suffer.

For the orphan it is a transformative process which becomes conscious through the individual experience and consequently appears in reality as individual accomplishment. This is in contrast to the purpose of any collective "box" which demands conformity depending upon directed thinking.[1] Therefore, the ambivalence inherent within the symbol is a threat to imposing uniformity. Modern institutions tend to misuse the term symbol. Their allegoric view of reality is served by a mechanistic-concretization based upon a search for causes. The full dynamism of the symbol is different since it leads to the question, "What ails me?"

Primarily the answer to the query has as many meanings as there are individuals who embrace a symbolic answer. Only traditional signs and allegories of logos are simple. A symbol does not define or explain. It simply yokes the subjective and objective levels of experience. For the orphan it points beyond itself to a meaning that is darkly divined yet still beyond one's cognitive grasp and cannot be fully expressed in the familiar logos of our language. The energetic value of the archetypal psyche is activated.[2]

Secondly, the Way of the Stone cannot be accomplished by intention and the will of the individual alone. It needs the dynamism of a symbol. It is immersion into a candescent process by the act of submission. "I will wash" means to purify the human intellect of its hubris whose reasoning always seeks to avoid unbearable paradox. The Way of the Stone is in contradiction to that grandiose state which assumes the intellect literally possesses the transcendent mystery by the power of its cognitive talents. Always taking one side of paradox precludes any symbolic view of itself suffering the consequences of being unconscious.[3] Therefore, its reaction is limited to a sense of being victimized.

Thirdly, the associated archetypal images that arise from yoking with an unconscious inner authority alter the nature of suffering. Self-revelation originating from the archetypal dimension has no bridge to the light of consciousness without the understanding and validation of mythological images. To submit is to realize that the universal structure of archetypes represents the typical experiences found in ordinary life. I thereby yoke my encounter with suffering from my son's passage to that mystery.

The archetypal mystery does not communicate the language of the conscious mind as logos. Its manifestation is possible only through the symbolic nature of metaphor or mythos. Therefore, we are freed from any exclusive intellectual formulation which gives a specific designation to a symbol transforming it into an allegory and used as spiritual or religious "symbols."

Symbols also serve us by revealing that the experience of suffering, weakness, and failure belong to an inner source, not just to the peripheral consciousness but to the "One who wills to suffer." It is the experience given to me by singing Christ's Hymn. It is the most universal mistake of the ego to assume total personal responsibility for all of its sufferings and failures.

During an active symbolic life there are certain "With- Out- Words" (W.O.W.) moments in time when the outer and inner experience of being are spontaneously united. This extraordinary instant of yoking is called synchronicity. The idea is to be available for those extraordinary moments by being conscious of that possibility.

8. I will be united and I will unite, Amen

The Discipline of Synchronicity

"This phenomenon consists of a symbolic image constellated in the psychic inner world, a dream, for instance, or a waking vision, or a sudden hunch originating in the unconscious, which coincides in a 'miraculous' manner, not causally or rationally explicable, with an event of similar meaning in the outer world."[1]

Synchronicity occurs in two aspects. An unconscious objective image comes into consciousness directly or indirectly through dreams, by centering meditation, or by spontaneous premonitions. An outer objective situation not causally related coincides with this content. As a single chance event it is always irrational, being of the Stone's mythos nature rather than logos of the Rock. The meaningful coincidence of these two events carries an energy which is described as numinous.

As a discipline this unification of the inner "I" and peripheral "I" is acknowledged as the experience of synchronicity. The occurrence is spontaneous and candescent, filling awareness with a sense of supernatural presence. This is an epiphany which carries an energy experienced as numinous. The individual feels the divine power of yoking in the flash of a moment. He or she is hit with energy. Unpredicted insights and creativity spontaneously arise.

The understanding of this phenomenon is clouded by strict adherence to the principle of causality which separates outer and inner events. This concept of linear sequence for time, before and after, cause and effect, exists in the scientific, rational domain of the peripheral "I." It is product of directed thinking which abhors the irrational and unpredictable. It is dependent upon a statistical perception of reality. Effects must have causes providing a separation of the inner authority "I" from the peripheral "I," divine and human experiences of life.

Synchronicity delineates to a moment in time where the inner sense of "I" and the peripheral sense of "I" are united. The dynamism of this union becomes spontaneously active, and freely creates numinous images beyond sensual perceptions of reality through dreams, visions, spontaneous fantasies, and physical symptoms. Myths represent the stories of those epiphanies and candescent moments of creativity arising from the depths of the archetypal psyche.

Because the union of the inner and outer "eye" produces synchronicity there are images with symbolic messages that spontaneously arise. This union frees us from the grip of grandiosity, since the peripheral "I" is no longer isolated by its one-sided concepts. The need to rationally control all experiences fades away to the candescence of an epiphany or profoundly humbling insight.

Synchronicity and serendipity are not the same. Serendipity occurs when two outer events come together, unexpectedly producing a favorable outcome while gratifying the desires of the ego. In contrast, synchronicity occurs as an unpredictable encounter between inner and outer dimensions.

Serendipity hinges on discovery while synchronicity provides the wisdom of revelation. So, it appears that serendipity is a separate or additional energy by which the psyche manipulates outer reality to achieve its hidden intention. The donkey-carrot tale suggests serendipity is a fortuitous coupling of two outer events supporting the desires and expectations of the ego, but at the same time secretly guiding it to fulfill unconscious designs.

As an example, during 1987 my life, as it had been, ended. My next action was energized with a "carrot" of financial rewards promised to me by a move to Austin. Texas. Two months after I made the move the carrot disappeared. Chaos ensued. Surprisingly, my future journey into the land of mythos became possible by wrestling with that unexpected adversity. The vanishing carrot had seduced me into a creative environment. One in which the dynamism of synchronicity first introduced me to Joseph Campbell and his Power of Myth.

It is evident that causality and linear time are yoked to a common wagon driven by the need for accountability. The straying Orphan is not one of its passengers. The Way of the Stone adds an alternative dimension of an "out of the wagon" experience capable of venturing into creative dimensions beyond rational accountability.

This errant process leads to a mystical destination and freedom accomplished by metaphorically departing from the collective wagon of causality and dogma, mounting an individual horse, leaving the logos path, and playfully galloping toward a horizon of creative breakthroughs introduced by synchronicities. Those chance epiphanies uniting both inner and outer realities are experienced simultaneously.

9. A lamp am I to you who perceive me, Amen

The discipline of wisdom from Dreams is an activity whereby candescence comes from an activity commonly manifested in dreams. When understood in the context of symbolic images, "A lamp glimmering in the darkness of sleep shows the way to wisdom. Lamp symbolism is linked to that of diffusion of light—candescence. It is the framework for light, and the light is a manifestation of the lamp. From this union derives the "one-ness" of the one. It is the summons for the invisible to take visible form."[1]

Jung distinguished between the prospective function of dreams and their negative or positive compensatory function. The latter means that the unconscious, considered relative to consciousness, adds to the conscious situation of all other elements of the previous day which remain subliminal because of repression. The prospective dream is anticipation in the unconscious of future conscious achievements.[1]

My previous orientation for wholeness, largely influenced by Jung, has focused on the transcendent function rather than the transcendent state. I know of many who have discovered refuge in this state of transcendence, but the Orphan Stone is not drawn to this Eastern Oriental experience of imminence or mystical ecstasy that inspires so many. Instead, its intention is focused on the transformation of the personality in the field of opposites and transcendent function, essential for the Orphan Stone, by accepting the wisdom within dreams and active or passive imagination.

It is then that Symbolic wisdom emanating from the inner "I" during dreams flows into our awareness. They are captured in the dawning zone just before the full light of awakening from sleep, or other altered states of consciousness, and before being interrupted by the mundane thoughts of daily living. The immediate act of journaling hinders their withdrawal into the depths of darkness, the unconscious. When retained, they freely gift me with "Sleeping Wisdom," rewarding my efforts to retain and creatively "play" with the messages. Their messages come to awareness in the language of symbolic images and related feelings.

Samuel Taylor Coleridge expresses this discipline beautifully:

> What if you slept,
>> And what if in your sleep you dreamed,
>> And what if in your dream you went
>> To heaven
>> And there you plucked a strange and

Beautiful flower
And what if when you awoke
You had the flower in your hand?
Oh, what then?

With that question the discipline of reflection is activated.

10. A mirror am I to you that know me, Amen

The Discipline of Reflection

It is a fearful experience to face the consequences of an unconscious drive for creative change. Jung classifies it as an instinct in humans. The anguish I suffer from autonomous disruptive events present me with a paradox. Kyle's death has presented me with this challenge. Am I to be caught up in unrelenting grief and let it rule my life? That which rules me becomes my wound that will not heal. Or do I submit to the Way of the Orphan Stone? The better choice implies that I have the opportunity for redemption by objective reflection.

"It is indeed wonderful to see how man, besides his life in the concrete, always lives a second life in the abstract. In the former he is abandoned to the storms of reality and to the influence of the present; he must struggle, suffer, and die like an animal. But his life in the abstract, as it stands before his rational consciousness, is the calm reflection on his life in the concrete and the world in which he lives...Here, in the sphere of calm deliberation, what previously possessed him completely and moved him intensely appears to him cold, colorless and for the moment, foreign and strange; he is a mere spectator (mirror looker) and observer. In respect of this withdrawal into reflection, he is like an actor who has played his part in the scene and takes his place in the audience until he must appear again. In the audience he quietly looks on at whatever may happen, even though it be in preparation of his own death; but then he again appears onstage and acts and suffers as he must."[1]

"What ails me?" is a mirroring question. It is looking at my own sub-jective reactivity, a step essential for engaging the Way of the Orphan Stone. It is not meant to imply that something is wrong with me, but to introduce objectivity freed from my emotions.

We all know about suffering. In contrast there must be an equal knowl-edge about how not to suffer. Otherwise one is irreversibly cast in the lot of a victim. In the Orphan Stone Way I have found several clues alluding to the purpose of my existence as it relates to suffering. Jung provides us with a clear explanation.

"The realization of why you suffer would not be possible unless there were that Archimedean point outside, the objective standpoint of the Self, from which the ego can be seen as a phenomenon. Without the objective standpoint of the Self the ego would remain caught up in hopeless sub-jectivity. But if you can see and understand your suffering without being subjectively involved, then, because of your altered standpoint, you also understand "how not to suffer."[2]

Through this altered standpoint provided by yoking, standing in relationship of one's non-ordinary reality, it is possibly to view a state of non-suffering. The inner authority becomes manifest in the human act of reflection; logos yoked with mythos. It is the process of human reflection whereby the divine descends to unite with the human and the human ascends to yoke with the divine. The inner "I" mirrors the peripheral "I" as an instrument of gnosis. A change in attitude is brought about whereby the individual personality bridges the disassociation between the two.

"Mirrors as reflecting surfaces indicate the discipline of speculation, revealing the wealth of symbolism relating to wholeness. The mirror is even called "the symbol of symbolism itself." The task of the mirror is not simply to reflect an image; it also becomes a part of that image and through it becoming a part, undergoes transformation. There is a rela-tionship between the object contemplated and the mirror which reflects it. This meaning makes the mirror a symbol of reciprocal awareness, Mys-tic consciousness."[3]

So, the wisdom made available by the Orphan Stone is activated by experience, and given meaning primarily by a reflective state of being. It is the capacity of engaging inner archetypal images and accepting their potential for healing insights. This activity is metaphorically experienced by participating in the disciplines of Christ's Round Dance.

"The Christ, or the self, is a "mirror": on the one hand it reflects the subjective consciousness of the participant, making it visible to him, and on the other hand it "knows" Christ. That is to say it does not merely reflect the spiritual man, it also reflects as (transcendental) whole."[4]

Through the candescence of reflectivity you will be entertained and inspired by the voices and performances of renowned mythological celebrities, their plights interfacing with the mystery of suffering in the realm of mortal fates, giving answers for the basic questions of life. These mythos dramas are not just remote abstractions derived from the history of mythological writings, but are archetypal images and patterns of behavior actively participating in our daily living experiences.

To unlock the mystery aspect of symbolic reflection, we are obligated to activate the discipline of amplification.

11. A door am I to you that knock on me, Amen

The Discipline of Amplification

In order to escape the concretizing of symbolic images manifesting from mythical consciousness of the intermediate realm, it is an obligation to amplify them and extract multiple meanings. Otherwise, it is imprisoned by allegory in service to logical creeds and consequently stripped of its mystery. The door as a gateway symbolizes the scene of passing from one state to another, from one world to another, from the known to the unknown, from the profane to the sacred. To knock is to open that door.

Christ said, "Behold, I stand at the door and knock: if any man hears my voice and opens the door, I will come in to him and will sup with him and he with me."[1]

The discipline of amplification is opening the door for the meaning when the "inner authority" knocks. In hearing the knock from the archetypal psyche we are introduced to images that reveal an unmistakably mythological symbol. To sup with me requires they be amplified and examined for their unlimited symbolic context, the inborn language of the archetypal psyche. In this way it can be integrated. Otherwise the reductive process will lead the seeker away from The Way of the Stone and merely reinforce the one-sidedness of the outer "I."

We achieve those revelations by using amplification and symbolic reflection whereby we discover that the psyche and body suffer in tandem, and share mythological and psychological influences, each mirroring the other. This is a natural way of giving an illustrative representation of the psychophysical relationship. To access this source of wisdom our focus must be for the metaphorical and how it is directed toward primal images where content and form become identical. If we concede any of our power to the Way of the Stone, that feeling of power derives its effectiveness from a yoked capacity to be both physical and psychical. The wisdom of Sophia is activated.

One enters the pathway of communication between the conscious personality and the archetypal psyche thereby accessing an inner source of strength. As a function of "Becoming" the effort must serve to open this swinging door entering into the inner recesses of the soul, and also returning into outer conscious activity. It is not always a wise journey for everyone to undertake.

Therefore, I do not by force of will alone take myself or anyone else into this dark place unless invited or forced there by events in life. Kyle's death left me with a choice of how I should proceed, but not whether I should proceed. My choice is the Way of the Stone.

When life involuntarily casts an individual into tragic loss or crisis they are in transformative space. During the grief process their life is dismantled and miserable. Some individuals, unfortunately, never seem to finish with their grief, and the world never congeals satisfactorily for them.

Let me share another example with you. A sixty-year-old man attended one of my Jung Society classes entitled, "The Nature of Suffering." He came for the first time to a Jungian event at the insistence of his wife, a devotee of Jung. In a small circle we began the discussion of suffering and its relationship to the unconscious. At the beginning of the second session this timid college professor shared a dream that he experienced the night after the first class.

He said he was in a house that felt strange and unpleasant. He walked through a door that led down in to a basement. Going down the stairs into this darkened place he noticed a second door on the floor of the basement. Opening it, he encountered a foul stench and a cold deathly presence. Frantically closing the opening he fled in panic, awakening from the dream in a cold sweat.

With this dreaming message it was apparent that the unconscious (deep within the cellar) was dangerous for him. His wife wisely chose to accept that message. She indicated that she would continue her journey into the unconscious psyche without his companionship and he dropped out of the class.

When the timing is right for such a venture, entering this door initiates a process of conscious development which ultimately leads to oneness or wholeness. Paradox is no longer divisive, but can be seen as two aspects of the same thing. As a result of this illuminated state, fear and desire are weakened by objective reflection. In contrast to starvation, wisdom thrives, and life is nurtured by participating in the continuous unfolding reciprocal relationship between the dual qualities of paradox present in any one object of experience.

I no longer see myself as an isolated point on the periphery of the circle, but also as the One in the center. Only subjective consciousness is isolated, but when it relates to its centre it has entered through the swinging door leading into wholeness. Whoever joins the sacred dance sees him or herself in the reflecting centre where "purpose" replaces causality.

12. A way am I to you the wayfarer, Amen

The Discipline of Active and Passive Imagination

"Imagination is more important than knowledge."
— Albert Einstein

When imagination is active, Yoking unites the two aspects of "I" with the Self. The process is essentially a hermeneutics of symbols because it carries a meaning which transcends the simple data of experience and makes for symbolic truth. This implies a perception of reality on the plane of active Imagination, during which active dialogue can be implemented for a deeper experience of yoking.[1]

The imagination never functions in isolation of the two aspects of "I." Full understanding of imagination demands a delicate balance between these two aspects of the psyche. In the mythic experience: "just as the soul is independent of the material, physical body and intellective capacity for the act of receiving information, the soul is also independent as to its imaginative capacity and activity."

"Once the reality of the transpersonal center has been experienced a dialectic process between ego and Self can, to some extent, replace the previous pendulum swing between inflation and alienation. But the dialogue is not possible as long as the ego thinks that everything in the psyche is of its own making."[2]

Inflation of the ego occurs when it feels unrealistically important, becoming vain, pompous, and presumptuous. It is identified as the Self and becomes blown up beyond the limits of its proper size.

Alienation of the ego occurs when the yoking between the ego and the Self has been damaged. A symptom is the lack of self acceptance. The result is emptiness, despair, meaninglessness, and in extreme cases psychosis or extreme violence including suicide. The Wisdom of the Stone protects the orphan from possession by grandiosity, negative inflation, or alienation.

127

We thus have an intermediate world of the mystic beyond the control of our scientific mind. It is only available by imaginative function, and the events can be lived only with a consciousness capable of that activity. But, the participation in active imagination is a highly sophisticated process and can then only be effectively and safely done with assistance of a ritual elder.[3]

To integrate the figures of fantasy into practical application the individual actively participates in the disciplines of the yoking dance. Here the choice is highly individual. For some it is easiest to write them down. Some visualize them, and others draw or paint them with or without visualization. If there is a high degree of conscious cramp, often only the hands are capable of fantasy. They model or draw figures that are often foreign to the conscious mind.

To facilitate acceptance and activation of that "impossible" proposal of active imagination one is solicited to dance the dance. Dancing is an individual activity whereby the symptoms of suffering are converted into healing symbols by devoted attention to the Disciplines of the Sacred Dance.

The soul dance begins by featuring the individual experience and is independent of collective containment. As previously stated, it is the sacrifice of reductive thinking and submission to a creative process whereby suffering is confronted.

When one reads my *Caduceus: A Physician's Quest for Healing* it is apparent that the *Collected Works of Jung* and his disciples, the *Power of Myth* and other sources from Joseph Campbell, *The Dictionary of Symbols*, and *The American Dictionary* for language derivatives are the group of primary, repeated sources I utilized for amplification of the "Begetting" experience.

Summary of the Disciplines

The Way of the Stone is interpreted as my call for renewal. When cast astray by the activity of the trickster I seek the wisdom of Hermes. Within his circle of stones I listen patiently for a mystery beyond my personal subjectivity. In this sacred space I become attuned to the reality of the images as they appear and give value to their symbolic messages. It is a timeless moment in which I often feel the divine power of synchronicity. I record my dreams and acknowledge the light of wisdom they announce. In addition I seek reflective mirrors which reveal a wealth of symbolism related to my process of yoking. As a result I escape the limitation of allegory by amplification of meaning. And finally I encourage discourse or dialogue with the archetypal source at my centre, giving priority and validity to active imagination.

CHAPTER 9

MYTHOS OF SUFFERING

The Orphan Stone Way

Christ's Hymn has given me twelve ways to yoke my personal sense of grief to its archetypal origin. See what happens to my suffering during the process of Singing the Hymn and Dancing the Dance. Although it is impossible to relay to you the effect or feeling tone associated with the ritual there is a certain discourse that can be expressed. Continuing with the Hymn of Christ:

"Now as you respond to my dancing, behold yourself in me who speaks....

As you dance ponder what I do, for yours is this human suffering which I will you to suffer—for you would be powerless to understand your suffering had I not been sent to you as the logos by the Father.

If you understood suffering, you would have non-suffering. Learn to suffer, and you shall understand how to not suffer... understand the Word of Wisdom in me."[1]

My study of mythology taught me that suffering is a human fate and how to confront, bear, and interpret suffering. It has informed me that life is not life without suffering. Instead mythology teaches that suffering is a call for renewal. One biological law states that peace and harmony leads to complacency and complacency leads to the nonsurvival of the species.

Every step of the inner Way on the "yellow brick road" to the wisdom of the Orphan's Stone advances the wholeness of personality. The challenging distress is not a punishment or a moral issue. It is an indispensable means of leading one to a place where life intends to take him or her. The trickster is thereby given a positive value; suffering is defined accordingly. Repeating the poem,

"Your pain is the breaking of the shell
That encloses your understanding.
     Even as the stone of the fruit must break
That its heart may stand in the sun, so you must know pain.
     And should you keep your heart in wonder
At the daily miracles of your life, your pain
Would not seem less wondrous than your Joy."
                                    — Gibran, Kahlil, *The Prophet*, p. 52

The favored logos meaning for the word "suffer" is, "To feel pain or distress; sustain loss, injury, harm, or punishment, endure or bear. In general usage suffer is preferably used with *from*, rather than *with*."[2]

The mythos connotation for the meaning of suffer is symbolized by the Trickster which essentially alters the relationship from the passive victim, who struggles *from* a "problem of suffering," to the one who also has a conscious encounter *with* suffering revealing the mystery of his or her creative urges. Suffering *from* is a function of causality and empathy; suffering *with* is a manifestation of synchronicity and is accompanied by a feeling of compassion which appears to be a function of one's maturity and relationship with the Stone.

Because I am a devoted seeker on the Way of the Orphan Stone I am obligated to learn from my tragic times. It is on these occasions that I ask, "Who am I that all this should happen to me? What ails me?" In doing so I do not ask what is wrong with me? That train of thought entraps me with a moral dilemma and other emotional entanglements such as guilt, anger, and regret. According to the Stone I must subject those symptoms to the process of candescence rather let them unconsciously torture my life. I must have the discipline, patience and willingness to scrutinize and understand what is happening within my own soul.

Entering the process of yoking took me to the insights provided by Jung, "When the inner man wants something different from the outer man and we are at war with ourselves, only then in this situation of stress do we discover the psyche as something which thwarts our will which is incompatible with our conscious standpoint. We no longer deny the dark stirrings of the unconscious are active powers; that psychic forces exist which at present at least cannot be fitted into our rational order."[3]

To find the answer to my fateful question, "What ails me," I must enter into the world of my own mythos. It is here that I will encounter the dynamics of the archetypal trickster. In other words I discover that my subjective experience of suffering is the prime material; the work of redemption. After the initial wounding and emotional reaction, the inner activity of stone consciousness is activated and the ingredients of suffering undergo distillation. For the Way of the Stone this activity consists of twelve operations or disciplines which were covered in the last chapter.

To gain an archetypal understanding of personal suffering is difficult. It defies the limitations imposed by our cultural domination of causal concepts and associated subjective reactivity. This being the origin of creativity born of unresolved suffering, it produces great works of music, poetry and art. An artist when informed that meditation might take away his suffering may respond: "Absolutely not, it would mean sacrificing my capacity to be creative." I confess my suffering and acknowledge that my trials and suffering have given me the impetus to write this book.

"If you understood suffering, you would have non-suffering. Learn to suffer, and you shall understand how to not suffer."

Jung provides me with his insight. "The intellectual mind denies the genuine nature of suffering. Reductive thinking seeks to explain it rationally, the consequence of something secondary, denying the validity of the underlying archetypal dynamics. Rational formulas may satisfy the present and the immediate past, but not the whole of human experience. This can be accomplished only by the symbol which unites human experience with the entelechy of divine origin."[4]

Entelechy is a Greek word meaning true destiny. The symbol which unites human experience is suffering and is synonymous with symptoms.

You achieve "non-suffering" when you mobilize the capacity to participate in the dynamics of symbolization. The idea that tribulations are a siege upon whom or what you think you are signals the emergence of a chaotic force, the Trickster, an attempt to break through your attachments and heal you. "Therefore the attitude of the healer is less a question of a remedy and more the developing of the creative potential of the patient."

"The human and divine suffering set up a relationship of complementary and compensating effects. Through the Christ (Stone) symbol, man can get to know the meaning hidden within his suffering; he is on his way to knowing his wholeness. As a result of the integration, his ego (outer "I") enters the "divine" realm (inner "I") where it participates in "God's suffering." The drama of the archetypal life of Christ describes in symbolic images the events of conscious life—as well as the life that transcends consciousness—of man who has been transformed by his higher destiny."[5]

The word symbol means to throw together. It is insightful to recognize certain relationships. To throw a symbolic stone is the same as "kissing the wound," an emersion in life itself.

With trepidation, I ask, "What ails me?" If I am to investigate my thoughts, words and deeds, and if I seek to understand myself, it requires essential features, the Vessel of Hermes, the centre of integrating tendencies and healing defined as making whole. This active state allows me to objectively have it out with my own conflicts and emotions, instead of "innocently" suffering from them, while desperately searching for remedies.

"The realization of why you suffer would not be possible unless there were that Archimedean point outside, the objective standpoint of the Self, from which the ego can be seen as a phenomenon. Without the objective standpoint of the Self the ego would remain caught up in hopeless subjectivity. But if you can see and understand your suffering without being subjectively involved, then, because of your altered standpoint, you also understand "how not to suffer."[6]

Understand the Word of Wisdom in Me

By establishing the connection to my centre, I am able to restore contact with inner resources of strength and acceptance. When I become concerned with the everyday phenomena of life, the question of the purpose of symptoms is given equality to the search for cause and remedy. My personality is free to outgrow previous limitations of my ego. I notice that my personal agony is also impersonal and part of a greater sense of reality than given to me by causality. Yoking is to establish a stone bridge across the waters between two different worlds; causality and purpose.

The conscious interaction with my centre is a unifying and ordering principle. It is the archetype of wholeness. It is the source of life energy which unifies the various patterns and images activated by my life experiences. While I normally live in a dual world of "inner" and "outer" events, in a synchronistic world this duality no longer exists. Outer events behave as if they were a part of my psyche, so that everything is contained in the same wholeness.

In this way a different attitude is created, an attitude that accepts the irrational and the incomprehensible simply because it is happening. As previously noted, this attitude could be poisonous for a person who is already overwhelmed by the things that happen to him or her (victim). But it is the greatest value for one who selects, from all the things that happen, those experiences compatible with a progressive unfolding of his or her life. That activity of healing signifies a process of moving the victimized soul out of its stagnant backwaters and back into the flowing stream of life. Modern psychology is based on causality and cannot fathom the following possibility.

"The individual loses his guilt and exchanges it for an infantile innocence; no more can the adult blame the wicked father for this and the unloving mother for that, and all the time he is caught in this inescapable causal nexus like a spider's web, without noticing that he has lost his

134

moral freedom. But no matter how much parents and grandparents may have sinned against the child, the man "who is an adult" will accept these sins as his own condition which has to be reckoned with. Only a fool is interested in other people's guilt, since he cannot alter it. The wise man only learns from his own guilt. He will ask himself: Who am I that all this should happen to me? What ails me? To find the answer to this fateful question he will look within his own heart."[6]

My way of non-suffering in the face of suffering is to reap self-knowledge from the field of opportunities usually made barren by the chronic victim state of consciousness. This process is equivalent to placing my experience of grieving into the alchemical retort or hermetic vessel and then patiently waiting for a healing image, sometimes seen as the divine child, to emerge. If the child thrives, it would mean that the realization of the wholeness encompasses more and more of my life as an individual, attracting more and more vitality which permeates all facets of my conscious activity.

"That which one has not experienced does not exist." The following actual experience serves as an appropriate model to demonstrate the Way of the Stone.

The initiate stands before a kitchen window, observing the sunrise, feeling a dread for the arduous tasks promised by the impending day. At the same moment he is following his routine morning activity while taking vitamins, hoping they will in some way energize his mind and body. He is distracted by his own fatigue. While in the midst of swallowing them, he coughs and aspirates one large capsule into his lungs. The Trickster is active. His body as expected is mirroring the initiate's inner struggle.

The respiratory distress sends him to the hospital where the obstruction is removed, but unexpectedly the chest x-ray also reveals a nodule in the right upper lobe. After surgical resection of the nodule, the pathologist determines the nodule is benign, but of an undetermined identity. Consultations with experts in other medical centers also fail to identify its specific cell type.

Months later the initiate opts to consult an alternative doctor with his unresolved complaints of disabling post operative fatigue and a thirty pound weight loss. The cause and remedy are essentially undetermined by medical evaluations. My alternative medical appraisal also fails to uncover any organic abnormality. With this information, a door opens for introversion, and reflection upon non-traditional avenues of exploration. I ask him, "Have you experienced any vivid dreams recently or during this time of unexpected tragedy?"

Without hesitation he announces that during the fourth night postoperative, he lapsed into a five hour coma during which time he had the following vision:

He said, "It began with an entity coming forth as a guide into a journey which depicted a destructive war scene. On the streets of a city there were people being slaughtered by hidden snipers. The scene shifted to a cathedral where he knew he was looking into the face of eternity. The scene again shifted to a place where he was in a cocoon-like container with a single opening floating in space. Suddenly, outside the cocoon there appeared a threatening demonic creature attempting to enter and kill him. In a major panic he struggled to escape." At that moment he regained consciousness, shaky from the dream. The five-hour "coma" had no medical explanation.

I asked him what his life was like at the time. He informed me that he was married with two children and currently working as a property manager for his wealthy father-law, a retired minister. He had graduated from college with a bachelor's degree in psychology, but instead of entering a practice he became a manager of the father-in-law's real estate. Although this situation provided a job with financial security and a happy wife, he desperately struggled with the drudgery of his required daily work tasks and his confinement within a strict "religious environment."

If we accept the tenet that the unconscious aspect of Psyche acts as the creator of this entire drama, then there is a message and circumstances that demand "impossible tasks." He excitedly accepted the symbolic images of his medical experience as the ingredients of an initiatory ritual. He recognized his soul's desperate call for a life change. As a consequence of acting upon that revelation his dormant gift for creative imagination awoke in the apparent tragedy of his suffering and symptoms.

Briefly, let me recount the reality and the symbolism of the patient's plight. The symbolism of being choked by the aspiration of a vitamin (vita-life) during a routine activity, while looking out of a window beyond the kitchen (nurturing space) symbolic of his life situation. While so engaged, a severe life threatening respiratory distress led to the discovery of a neoplasm (new growth). This **did not fit the traditional** diagnostic medical model, but represented a different paradigm.

The post-op coma with its symbolic vision presented three separate but connected encounters. First his life was threatened by hidden villains symbolic of the Trickster at work. Secondly he experienced eternity and escaped from certain death symbolizing his escape from his previous life. Thirdly, the cocoon in which he exists symbolizes the persona which no longer perceived safety. The unconscious demonic forms threatened his life if he refused to respond to the call for change. The escape symbolizes rebirth from the coma of death.

After archetypal reflections and amplifications upon the patient's full drama, he grasped the necessity to alter his life. His numinous encounter became his transformative experience. At that moment he fully perceived the symbolic interpretations and their implications for him in the years to come. In short he submitted to his quest for self discovery during which a psychic potential was conceived. He initiated a transition by first becoming a massage therapist. Subsequently he quit his job and during that same year he was divorced which freed him to pursue his genius.

After responding to the symbolic images and answering their call for change, his fatigue subsided, while his weight loss and sense of physical well being returned. Actually it was energized by his transformative experience. He subsequently entered a progressive series of initiations by first becoming an advanced teacher in Tai Chi and **Qi**-Gong. He was initiated into Shamanism. More recently he became a certified practitioner of bio-feedback.

A whole world of creative imagination and healing opened up for him as he continued to explore his gifts and where they have led him. A plethora of mystical-shaman helpers, i.e., Fire Elk and White Buffalo Calf Woman, have come forth from the imaginal realm to guide and continually inspire him as his life experiences moves him further into a gratifying wholeness and feeling of well being. He had in his own way responded to the wisdom of his trickster. His submission to its purpose brought about his transformation from the common rock to a redeemed stone.

His medical history in terms of an alternative practice is one which validates the existence of an initiatory experience composed of the trickster, sacrificing the provisional life, and performing impossible tasks. The progressive initiations with helpers finally enacted a renewal of life. Being "tricked" by the demands for unrealized creativity is a life-threatening task, but it is also life "saving." The transition provides moments and stages in which authentic sacrifice of a most culturally valued state or persona is achieved. Transformation is demanded by the archetypal trickster for a continued vitality in his life.

Golden Years

What are the emotional consequences for a 78-year-old man who tragically loses his 29-year-old son? To this point in this book you have been given my response to that question. In more general terms the events of my golden years have kept me active in the gamesmanship of life. The context may change, but challenges continue to activate my ongoing transformational process.

The introspection of mythos keeps me from getting lost in the maze of personal retrospections typical of an aging thought process whereby a recall of lifelong events is limited to logos reconstruction of past events. The emotions associated with regret, guilt about the past, and fear of death are all too frequent. I have a more optimistic attitude. My daemon of creativity is not imprisoned by time bound memories. Instead, my errant way of "suffering with" my advancing years leads me to a mythos reflection upon my memoirs as well as my present experiences.

In contrast, what happens for the elderly individual when directed thinking is no longer astutely active, when the body demands increased support to survive, and when both are worn to a fragile state by the lifelong tedious work of survival plus the natural aging process? It would seem that the capacity for individual creative life is diminished. Those individuals exclusively guided by the rock often suffer from senility.

In contrast, the Stone is beyond the concepts of time and not similarly retired from life. Stone living just makes for foolishness. In the ordinary course of events the creative imagination of this archetypal orphan at my last stage of life is not consciously appreciated; chronic illness, senility and fear of death become an escalating burden.[7] The Trickster is encountered exclusively as an enemy without the seeming hope for psychical redemption.

Jung adds, "In primitive cultures we observe that the old people are almost always the guardians of mysteries and laws. Where is the wisdom of our old people, where are their precious secrets and their wisdom? For the most part our old people try to compete with the young.

Unfortunately not enough meaning and purpose for those who see in the approach of old age a mere diminution of life and can feel their earlier ideas only as something faded and worn out. We must not forget that only a few are artists in life; that the art of life is the most distinguished and rarest of all the arts. It is beyond the capacity of most people, particularly the educated part of humanity. That is the working of the intellect which tends to be diminished in the elderly mind and diminishes their active participation in modern life."[8]

Charles Schulz adds humor to this depressing subject:
Charlie and Lucy are standing together and Lucy asks, "Each stage of life seems to have its own special meaning. You hear about a lot of people talk about their golden years. Do you think there are golden years, Charlie Brown?
Charlie answers, "No I think they are more like copper."

Summary

The Way of the Orphan Stone suggests my personal rational process of grieving, and my realization must be symbolically yoked to an irrational mystery. My experience of suffering and my one-sided search for rational, consistent, logical meaning was incomplete for me. My conformation to orthodox thinking exclusively bound me to traditional meanings and robbed me of my uniqueness as an Orphan Stone.

I find it impossible to get a hold on the transcendent mystery by some cognitive act alone. I seem incapable of accepting a healing value for my experience and how it is connected to mythos. I conclude that "something is missing." My conclusions are vital to understanding the Way of the Orphan Stone. It is through the study of psychology and mythology that I have attained an awareness of the archetypal origins of suffering. Both my professional career and my personal life have in no small part contributed to that understanding.

Mythological themes lurk within the present day life of everyone, but typically their presence and pertinence are not appreciated by the logos directed mind. It is taboo. Therefore one becomes susceptible to drowning in a sea of grief or other emotions when surrounded by personal as well as public suffering. It is a fate imposed by irrational storms where the rational solutions imposed by the Rock fail to provide healing. By contemplating the imagery of myths I awaken to renewed potentials for my own life.

"I had always worked with the temperamental conviction that at the bottom there are no insolvable problems, and experience justified me in so far as I have often seen patients simply outgrow a problem that had destroyed others. This "outgrowing," as I formerly called it, proved on further investigation to be a new level of consciousness. The unsolvable problem lost its urgency. It was solved logically on its own terms, but faded out when confronted with a new and stronger life urge. It was not repressed and made conscious, but merely appeared in a different light, and really did become different."[9]

When the Rock's logical way of knowing becomes a "rocky road," as it frequently does over time, then an avenue paved with Stones of symbolism is available by asking, "What ails me?" It provides a pathway to the realization of those meanings least receptive to the vast majority who are at "home" with ready made, habitual patterns for interpreting the nature and meaning of their suffering.

The Art of Suffering

Engages the mystery of symbolism
  Thereby activating the vitality of psychic energy
Redefines the nature of creativity
  Thereby knowing the influence of a secret archetype
Activates the experience of synchronicity
  Thereby the mundane and divine are felt as one
Awakens a sense of being centered
  Thereby finding peace in the midst of chaos
Stimulates the activity of creative imagination
  Thereby images become a way of knowing
Invigorates the essence of compassion
  Thereby escaping the grip of one-sided concepts
Illuminates a true source of healing
  Thereby dancing to the rhythm of the soul
Births the healer within
  Thereby symptoms become symbols
Reaps self-knowledge from the field of opportunities
  Thereby the victim is offered redemption

The Wisdom of the Stone given to the errant orphan is simply one way amongst the vast accumulated strategies recorded during human-kind's historic struggle to survive omnipresent adversity and suffering. Certainly there are "different strokes for different folks."

Say not, "I have found the truth," but
Rather "I have found a truth."
Say not, "I have found the path of the soul."
Say rather, "I have met the soul walking
Upon my path, for the soul walks upon all paths."
The soul walks not upon a line,
Neither does it grow like a reed.
The soul unfolds itself, like the lotus of
Countless petals."
— Gibran, Kahlil, The Prophet, p. 54

141

LEVEL FOUR

TO SOPHIA'S WISDOM

Wisdom brings up her own sons'
And cares for those who seek her

For though she takes him first through winding ways,
Bringing fear and fairness to him,
Plaguing him with her discipline until she can trust him,
And testing him with her ordeals,
In the end she shall lead him back to the straight road.
And reveal her secrets to him.

— Ecclesiasticus, 4: 11-21, Jerusalem Bible

CHAPTER 10

VISION QUEST

Yoking Ritual

D ances in traditional cultures all have as their subject matter the changes experienced by people throughout their lives; rites of passage for changes that occur as people mature from childhood to old age. The sacred nature of ritualistic dance celebrates the seasonal cycles and enacts archaic stories, passing down traditional wisdom from generation to generation. However, the ritual is also an activity useful for enactment of a personal myth. The process of yoking indicated by the Hymn is a map for guiding one on the Way of the Orphan Stone, but the experience itself imparts a deeper meaning often discovered while exploring that personal myth.

Jung states, "In psychology one possesses nothing unless one has experience it in reality. Merely intellectual understanding is not sufficient. It supplies us only with verbal concepts, but does not give us their true content, which is to be found in living experience of the process as applied. We would do well to harbor no illusions in this respect: no understanding by means of words and no imitation can replace actual experience."[1]

Last year, I decided to walk my talk and enacted my investigation into suffering by activating the Round Dance ritual. The Dance focuses attention upon the inner reaches of the soul, yoking it with an outer sense of I. By actively engaging the twelve disciplines and the field of the Stone process, the dance took its effect in the field of consciousness. I assumed the role of the solitary one who becomes capable of "knowing" the Stone through the ritual.

145

This was achieved by yoking the state of the Orphan with the dynamism of primordial images as archetypes. Next I recorded my experiences as they were spontaneously activated. I noticed that when the Round Dance was enacted, it stimulated the onset of a transforming process of the Stone Ritual in my experience. The following introductory five lines from the Hymn set the stage for performing the ritual.

> Grace paces the round, I will blow the pipe,
> Dance the round all, Amen.
> The twelve paces the round aloft, Amen
> To each and all it is given to dance, Amen
> Who would not the dance mistakes the event, Amen

What follows is a view of my actual experience of the Round Dance. It is the fall season of 07; the first draft of my original manuscript "Drama Illuminati" was finished, but felt incomplete. "Something was missing." Whilst in the midst of this intuitive dilemma as a reflective quandary, the Way of the Stone responded. It revealed the prospect of a future serendipitous event.

My shamanic mentor and brother, Jerry Casebolt, issued the summons for a sweat lodge for the month of October. At the moment I received it I felt a quickening and immediately responded with an enthusiastic "yes!" In the same breath I thought, why not add a three day Vision Quest for inspirational insights into the origin of my feelings. I wanted to ritually ask about the uncertainty, "What ails me?" This was in relationship to my uneasiness about my manuscript, the "Drama Illuminati." For this purpose I decided to implement the Round Dance as the ritualistic method needed to enact my quest for a redemptive vision, hoping to attain some degree of freedom from my current discontent.

I asked myself the question; what will the yoking Dance awaken in me? To prepare for the vision quest and the anticipated answer I needed to consciously sacrifice food and physical comfort during a planned isolated, solitary experience. I selected my clothing in anticipation of warm days and very cold nights, with plenty of liquids, and readying myself for fasting. Anticipating fulfillment of my intent I had prepared a hard copy of the manuscript. Pleased with myself, I chuckled. I gathered my camping gear from its dusty abode and sorted through my accumulated "stuff" in order to recover what I anticipated would be needed.

The Sweat Ritual was scheduled for the coming Sunday evening, so I ventured to my special questing site on the preceding Thursday afternoon. It is situated at the edge of a dry-creek bed surrounded by a forest of a variety of young and old trees. Divination of the area brought me to a spot where many years ago I had done a similar Vision Quest.

Happy to be far from the distracting energy of the city, I quickly began preparation of the site. I gathered firewood and stones for the central fireplace and outer circle. A small still voice of warning stopped me in my tracks. A sense of err gave an ominous feeling. In a flash of insight I "knew" I was an uninvited intruder. I had not asked the residing spirits for permission to be there. I was trespassing in their domain.

At the moment of this knowing pause I became quiet and centered. I then petitioned for their permission and blessing. A tall scraggy old Indian man appeared just east of my site. He was dressed with a ragged old shirt, patched and torn britches. Barefooted, his long gray hair flowed wistfully in the breeze as it touched his ancient wrinkled face.

With a gruffly frown he loudly announced, "I am Little Wolf. You are trampling around in my Forest!"

I respectively bowed. "Most wise one, many years ago you permitted my presence in this forest when I was introduced to you by the Shaman, Jerry. As before, I humbly request your permission to perform a three day sacred ritual within the confines of your most hallowed space."

He stood in silent repose with a quizzical countenance that encouraged me to continue my plea.

"I respectively submit that my intentions are honorable and sacred. I will limit my presence by marking the boundary of my space with stones and only perform my ritual within it. The forest spirits are invited to witness, but are to remain outside its boundaries. They are not to interfere thereby allowing me to perform the rituals of my Sacred Dance in peace. I also ask for your permission to gather stones and fallen wood for the fire. It is my desire to perform a meditative circular dance. In three days I will do a sweat lodge with Shamans Jerry and John and then I will respectively depart from your domain in peace."

Hesitating thoughtfully, his resisting frown slowly transformed into a receptive smile, He answered, "You have three suns and three moons."

"Little Wolf, thank you for your kindness," I replied.

The crisp, cold air invigorating both mind and body, I now felt at peace as I returned to my preparations. The first chore was to establish the center with a fireplace of stones. The second was to search for twelve medium sized stones, the ones I could easily carry. I placed them in a circle around the center, each stone equidistant from the center and from each other.

Then I squared this circle with logs procured from the floor of the surrounding forest. By nightfall all the physical preparation was complete. I ignited the central fire. Surveying the scene I saw that all was in place. I felt deeply gratified to be in the midst of the forest's natural beauty. While resting in reverent silence I relished a cup of warm soothing tea.

My body felt comfortable. I had on a short sleeved shirt when the daytime temperature was in the low 80's. But now with the sun completely set the temperatures began to drop rapidly to the high 40's and absolute darkness surrounded the fire lit circle. In this serene stillness with escalating coldness and physical fatigue, I felt the urge to retreat to the warm confines of my soft sleeping bag for the night and in that space relished the feeling of a much needed rest before entering into the dreamtime. I felt gratified. The spirits were pleased. My soul was at peace.

I awakened in the middle of the night to pass water. Where am I, I asked myself; in another world? Every tree, rock, and occupant of the forest was bathed with a soft, illuminating light. Above me was a moon in all its full glory. I was enthralled, filled with awe by witnessing this amazing synchronistic moment. What a marvelous gift of sacred experience had become mine to share! I wondered why I had not anticipated such an auspicious event. The fullness of the moon mesmerized me. In this altered state I was absorbed in her serene ambiance.

In deep reflection, I wondered if there was some mysterious insight to be gained by my mental oversight. The thought mingled with reverence adding depth to my spontaneous awe. Its luminosity engendered an aura and a moment of sacred inspiration. While in the midst of my reflection on this mystery, under the nocturnal moon, I compassionately eased back into the sanctuary of dreamtime. Upon awakening in the morning my first thought was more of a question than of some profound revelation. Was that awesome experience actual or had it been a dream?

I embraced the coming day. I bathed in the warm air and brightness of the midmorning Sun. I commenced the ritual process, as an experience of "two-ness." I placed my hands over my heart and contemplated its attributes: compassion, innate harmony, healing presence and unconditional love. I experienced a full sense of innate harmony, the quiet stillness within my soul in the presence of healing images. I felt content and receptive to any message that might come my way.

With my heart centering ritual complete I prepared to dance. Within the circle of the twelve disciplines I recited the hymn of Christ by chanting one discipline repeatedly during each of twelve rounds.

> I will be saved and I will save, Amen.
> I will be freed and I will free, Amen
> I will be wounded and I will wound, Amen
> I will be begotten and I will beget, Amen.
> I will eat and I will be eaten, Amen.
> I will be thought, being wholly spirit, Amen
> I will be washed and I will wash, Amen.
> I will be united and I will unite, Amen

A lamp am I to you that perceive me, Amen
A mirror am I to you that know me, Amen.
A door am I to you that knock on me, Amen.
A way am I to you the wayfarer, Amen.

Twelve rounds completed one Dance. At that point I comfortably seated myself with my manuscript and a pencil in hand under the warm rays of the Sun. I briefly contemplated upon my quandary over the Illuminati manuscript.

The following comments are an accounting of the three levels of light I had realized within the context of my vision quest. They revealed the contents that were to be sacrificed and replaced by those new contents that needed to be further explored.

One: The forest and my sacred place were enlightened by the pleasant warm rays gifted by the Sun. With the spirit of logos I began an examination of my script. Other than an occasional pause for stretching, drinking fluids, or restful contemplation, I stayed engrossed in my task; actively rewriting some, rearranging others, and extracting a great deal of unnecessary material. The original manuscript transformed before my eyes. I was in a different time of being in this different space. My intuition toyed with the imagery I experienced during daylight. By evening I had completed editing about one-half of the manuscript. It was a different time in sacred space, lasting as an act of sacrifice, the gift of contact with my inner Self. The emergence of differing ideas significantly transformed my transcript.

Two: As the Sun completed its journey beyond the western horizon its enlightening influence subsided. The air rapidly became cooler. All was dark by seven P.M. I ignited the fire at the center of the circle for light and warmth. All the surrounding forest was in absolute darkness. The only visible things were within the perimeter of the sacred circle. I realized I was witnessing the "enlightenment" of the central fire. Without the light of that fire I would be in total cold darkness. Surely this state of the forest represented the experience the mystics call the "dark night of the soul." I repeated the heart center ritual and followed it with twelve more rounds of the circular dance.

Seated within the ambiance of sacred ritual I focused upon the flames. I felt a deep awareness of the liberating quietude of innate harmony. My imagination turned the simple flame into a Promethean Fire. The warm introversion of thought forms crept into the inner reaches of my soul.

Three: I allowed the fire to burn out. The moon shone in the "fullness of full." It illuminated the forest with paradisiacal candescence. After eleven P.M. I performed the meditative circular dance. A pleasant fatigue encircled me like a mother's arms. My soul and spirit took rest together in a lunar embrace. I focused my attention on the larger illuminated surroundings. I felt united in heart and soul with this amazing display of lacy shadows and glistening tree trunks, all present with a mysterious luminosity. Was the radiance emanating from the darkness? I couldn't tell. Entranced by the mysteriously slow motion dance, I observed images within images, black shadows encased in golden fringes, intermingling with a maze of fractal patterns, the things between things.

When the moon eventually reached its pinnacle it was immediately above the sacred circle. An opening in the forest canopy allowed the ritual circle to be clearly and fully illuminated. The shadow world was indiscriminate. With a reverent feeling of gratitude for this illuminating adventure in this hallowed place, I succumbed to the circadian call for sleep. The moon's mythos lingered in my thoughts. I felt a sense of gratitude for the experience of the radiance within darkness, a gleaming treasure beyond the "day" of enlightenment, the dark night of the soul and familiar vocabulary of logos dependent upon intelligence quotient.

I awoke the next morning realizing that the previous drama of synchronistic experiences would be repeated. This time I embarked into the ritual with active aware participation and deepening union with the mystery of darkness and light. Illumination had attained a mystical meaning. I reflected on the mystique of the overall experience. I thought about the modern development of artificial light. Then I contrasted technology's so called advances with the experiences of the earlier humans who were illuminated by the sun, moon, and fire. Not only had I intellectually seen the difference, I experienced it. It was a new awareness of the need to unite thinking with feeling for which nature's candescence is a proper metaphor.

I began the second day by repeating the sacred round dance. Then, in the full light of a bright sun, my mind returned to the printed pages of the Illuminati manuscript. I realized that I was still enchanted by the magnetic mystique of "moon illumination." While in the bright daylight of intellectual discrimination I shifted to the spirit of logos and continued editing the remaining half of the original composition. Its contribution to clarity served to improve the quality of my writing. As I proceeded it occurred to me that I was essentially rewriting my book.

A shamanic voice from within spoke and suggested I change the title to: *Way of the Orphan Stone.* The Hymn and Dance then became the central activity, and exemplified my experience of Hermetic containment in Sacred Space.

Cold darkness embraced the fading daylight. The first beams of moonlight penetrated the forest canopy. It was time for another round dance. I sang the hymn that ignites the "inner fire."

Fatigued, I sat quietly focused on the fire's radiant flames. The warmth and light gave me a sense of peace. The cold darkness prevailed, but its stillness came alive with a bright inner central light reflecting the outer fire. I focused upon its flames and the energy of its warmth. The "other" worldly experience was a repetition of the previous night with one important difference.

Sacred Teachers

Out of the interlacing shadows of moonlight stepped a smiling elderly woman. She took my hand. There was a special energy in her hand that gave me a warm feeling of trust. We spontaneously embraced. I was immediately consumed by another worldly epiphany. I felt I was in the loving arms of Sophia. The scenery changed. We were walking together on a rocky trail leading into an ancient cave. Its irregular stone structure, many interconnecting chambers, and its open apertures gave me the feeling of touching raw nature. Entering the central chamber Sophia, the wise old woman, turned to me. She pointed to an altar. On it was a slender golden chalice and a black mask.

She said to me, "These sacred symbols are your teachers."

While I was in the process of giving my full attention to the golden chalice and black mask she vanished. In this sacred space I was enthralled with a spontaneous sense of wonderment that turned to a feeling of uneasy curiosity.

Upon my return to ordinary reality, reflecting and journaling, I wrapped words around the mythos of my experience. I had to process the meanings of the symbolic images.

The chalice, within the context of the mystery of begetting suggests the Cup or the Holy Grail. The image relates to achieving success. Further amplification revealed a deeper mystery. The Bible stresses that the cup is a symbol of human destiny. Individuals being allotted their fate by God receive the cup and its mysterious contents and its potential message of hope for human understanding.

"When Jesus took sup from the cup, it was not simply his death to which he referred, but to his destiny which God offered him. He accepted his fate with true knowledge of its divine purpose in the spirit of submission. As the Grail it is both vessel and book, thus confirming the two fold meaning of what it contains; revelation, destiny and nature of life."[2]

Throughout history the mask has symbolized many diverse meanings which depend upon the cultural context. Since the mask in my dream has a generic appearance and is black, it suggests the dynamism of a hidden shadow. The meaning is specifically revealed through the dynamism of the Orphan Stone. What is the mythos wisdom of the mask?

"Masks are designed to subjugate and control the invisible world. These forces move about in so many different shapes as to explain the varied combinations of carved human and animal figures unendingly and sometimes monstrously intertwined. It is the participation in a mystical experience and ethnologists have, in any case, already compared the use of masks with the practical methods of access to the mystical life."[3]

The mythology of rituals informs us that a mask transforms the one who wears it, leading to an altered state. Thereby it gives the strength or power of what it represents by making one no longer human. In this state one is given access to new worlds or experiences that cannot be ordinarily reached.

The potential wisdom inferred by the symbolism of the chalice and mask comes from the meaning it has for the Way of the Stone. When I acknowledged the role of the trickster the mystical meaning of life and death became my greatest teacher of wisdom. At this time I honored Sophia and her visionary revelation of the chalice and mask.

Being in rhythm with the Round Dance refers to the yoking of the outer and the inner sense of "I." My most recent nocturnal dream experience became a practical reality because I accepted its dream-like strangeness. I acknowledged that lunacy has teaching value. The dynamic tension of its metaphoric meanings serves to take me into the world of wonder, awe, perplexity, and reveals an essential sense of truth or beauty beyond any ordinary awareness and expectations.

I accepted that my inner authority contained the message which potentially infused my life with unconditional joy. At the same time my linear daytime of conditional rationality was disrupted by the threatening activity of the Trickster. Its "destructive" intentions presented me with suffering and death as a contradiction to my sentient and stable sense of being. I discovered the chalice and its contents, alchemically wrought with glowing outcomes, were paradoxically hammered into the sword of duality. I must also accept the blessings of death.

Now I am in the third day. It is a time in the Quest process when I must become a good custodian of nature. The last of my three days was lapsing into the common reality of ordinary life. It is proper to leave the site as I originally found it, without residual personal effects. The exception was the placement of the resident stones. My inner message was that they were to remain in their configured arrangement as a continued monument for the ritual. I paused, centered, and silently expressed my appreciation to the resident spirit for his gift of a sacred place. I bid Little Wolf farewell in a quiet sacred way. Those conciliatory duties respectfully completed, I prepared to join my brothers in preparation for a sweat lodge.

What followed was my sweat lodge ritual of gratification. I blessed the gifts received while performing the sacred dance in the circle. Entrance into the hallowed space of the sweat lodge requires the rituals of cleansing the body, mind, and spirit. I enacted it in the spirit of reverence and humility. The sweat lodge represents the ancient configuration of an archetypal pattern exemplified by the Mandala. Communication in the sweat lodge is done in the same manner as the Round Dance. It is an expression of wholeness. Wholeness then is a practical definition of healing in sacred space. For me it was a continuation of my dance with Sophia.

In a circumambulating order each brother voices those matters of value or concern for his soul and shares his gifts of vision. At this concluding stage of my quest, my sense of presence in the lodge was dominated by personal feelings of gratitude for the total quest experience. The sacred sharing among my fellow Orphans present in the lodge united me with an ancient brotherhood, each "known" by their individual and unique Way of the Stone.

Unbeknownst to me my previous efforts to cloak the process as an Illuminating Drama were appropriate for the ritual process of the vision quest, but not the manuscript. Also emerging during the Vision Quest I recognized there are three metaphoric levels of illumination interacting as one process in achieving the Way of the Orphan Stone. Added to Logos and Mythos I now feel the inner fire of Eros.

Awakening Eros

To introduce the Eros process I was reminded of a *Peanuts* cartoon by Charles Schulz. Lucy, decked out in her baseball gear, approaches Charlie Brown, and says:

"Well Charlie Brown, here I am ready to start a new season. I am very optimistic about our chances this year and full of enthusiasm. By the way, are you going to be our manager again?"

Charlie responds, "Yes, I guess I am."

Lucy with a frown states, "I'm very pessimistic about our chances this year and suddenly I've lost all of my enthusiasm."

Lucy's loss of enthusiasm and energy appears to be related to management from an outer source of "authority." The process of introversion during the Round Dance connects the orphan with an inner sense of guidance, a source of energy. This psychical energy, creativity, and authority are activated by Eros, the experience of being alive.

Joseph Campbell tells us, "People say that what we are seeking is a meaning for life. I don't think that is what we are really seeking. I think that what we are really seeking is an experience of being alive, so that our life experiences on the purely physical plane will have resonances within our own innermost being and reality, so that we actually feel the rapture of being alive."[4]

Eros, or libido, in the examples above refers to the symbol which is the carrier of psychic energy as active enthusiasm rather than being limited to sexual connotations. But what does that inference mean in practical terms? I determined that the task becomes one of wrapping words around the mythos of Eros to a related source of energy or "management." By doing so, our subjective experience of suffering or pleasure becomes related to the content of circumstances and thus energized with feeling and insight activated by the symbolic meaning of Eros.

"It is a generally recognized truth that physical events can be looked at in two ways: from the mechanistic and from the energetic standpoint. The mechanistic view is purely causal: it conceives an event as the effect of a cause, in the sense that unchanging substances change their relationship to another according to fixed laws. The energetic point of view on the other hand is essentially final. Final is used to avoid the misunderstanding that attaches itself to the common conception of teleology; mainly that it contains the idea of an anticipated end or goal."[5]

The idea of finality has to do with an understanding related to symbolic meaning and purpose, thus a means to an end. Rather than a search for causes, it gives attention to the movement of energy. The activated Eros as psychic energy, functions in service to a transformational process which challenges the status quo of one's existing personality. It requires a point of view that accepts the validity of inner "management" as an archetypal source. In my vision quest I had danced to the hymn of introspection by application of the twelve disciplines in search for meaning when later learning of my son's death.[6]

Igniting the fire of Eros and radiating in its warmth, the third illuminating experience stimulates a process of transformation whereby the combination of logos and mythos takes form in service to the Way of the Orphan Stone.

In the evolution of the Greek gods, Eros follows Chaos, an opening in life in which Eros can appear and do his work. Eros as Hermes is ever near his source of authority in Chaos who as the Trickster threatens order and structure. This intimate relationship of Eros and Chaos appearing unexpectedly at the center of an ordered life implies a new order and predicts an initial breakdown of the old order.

A corked bottle, the structure which provides the concepts that define one's way of life and sense of well being is opened by Chaos, the Trickster. This event releases the psychical energy of Eros previously residing in the unconscious. The metaphoric implication of uncorking the bottle is the release of previously unconscious aspects of the personality, "inner man," which in its threatening voice demands a creative response from the "outer man." Simply put, the Way of the Stone demands a yoking of the outer authority to its inner authority driven by Eros.

The typical response to such an experience is the application of logos terminology. The emotional impact of being informed that you have a life threatening event or incurable disease is perceived as the loss of things or individuals to which one is deeply attached. Therefore, according to the modern paradigm, you punish it; you are at war with it, because it tortures you. That type of reactivity fosters a state of alienation whose accompanying violence is projected into outward experience, i.e., aggressive behavior, and imprisonment, or suffered inwardly as inflammatory disease and hospitalization.

Way of the Orphan Stone: the literal destructive threat of Eros is countered by mythos reflection which takes the compensatory Eros of rage and guilt back to its archetypal origin, thus avoiding the implied literal consequences. It is taken back to the archetypal source where it is transformed by the action of yoking. A process whereby those factors conceived as conflicting opposites, i.e., logos and mythos, come together within the mystical vessel of wholeness.

Within the darkness of the orphan experience of isolation is a revelatory candescence invisible to daylight vision or moonlight imagery alone. However, by introversion it is igniting the fire of enthusiasm as creative action is set in motion and relates to Eros as a source of energy and authority. In the midst of apparent chaos, disruption of predictability or continuity, those ambiguities disrupt any state of happiness. One learns that within the darkness of chaos there is redemption.

Post Script

My lifelong quest for healing has challenged me repeatedly through encounters with adversity or danger. Facing those chaotic times was like a brush with death. Eros, over time, has evolved into what I now identify as the Way of the Orphan Stone. The amplification of its personal meaning has instilled in me a profound awareness of mysterious inner forces. But will it survive the devastating test? With Kyle's death the integrity of my devotion, as well as my confidence in the Way of the Orphan Stone, have received their ultimate challenge. Am I to be rendered helpless, locked in unending regret and grief, or do I Dance to the Hymn of the Stone process making it my way to redemption?

As previously stated, the Way of the Stone does not take away my human tears, and solace from comforting hugs and human things. But over the course of time it prompts me to place my emotions in an alchemical retort, a place of candescence. It is a process of looking at my pain, looking completely within. Asking, "What ails me?" I submit my grief to an authority whose healing objectivity is related to the greater mystery of archetypes.

"The hidden word of God corresponds to the Gnostic myth of Sophia, a personification of the Word of God. In the process of creation, the divine wisdom, descended into matter; and then in the course of that descent she became lost and imprisoned in matter, then becoming the hidden word of God which is to be released and redeemed.

Psychological development in all its phases is a redemptive process. The goal is to redeem by conscious realization, the hidden Self, hidden in conscious identification with the ego. The dialogue of individuation is not possible as long as the ego thinks that everything in the psyche is of its own making. For modern man, a conscious encounter with the autonomous archetypal psyche is the equivalent to discovery of God."[7]

The overwhelming grief presented to me by the unexpected loss of Kyle would be redeemed by the mythos of his shining Chalice and mysterious Mask. His archetypal Eros has stimulated the creativity of this book and transformed the Elder into A Wise Old Fool.

CHAPTER 11

THE CHALICE AND MASK

The "Chalice" of life and the "Mask" of death have been and continue to be my principle teachers of wisdom, bearers of candescence. They are personifications of Sophia's hidden wisdom. It is a Way whereby the drama relating to Kyle's death has drawn me further into a longing for those archaic ideas which will redeem my grief.

> Tell a wise man, or else keep silent
> Because the mass man will mock it right away
> I praise what is truly alive,
> What longs to be burned to death.
>
> And so long as you haven't experienced
> This: to die and so to grow
> You are only a troubled guest
> On the dark earth
> — Bly, Robert, *Holy Longing, News,* 1970

It is fascinating to reflect upon my recent October Vision quest. I danced the dance. I walked the walk. I sang the Prayer. It brought forth a crucial change in the focus of journaling my experience. The spotlight centered upon the Way of the Orphan Stone. It became the primary archetypal profile for understanding my lifelong quest for healing. All other relevant archetypal ideas were considered and filed away, because they were secondary to the purpose of my quest for the Orphan Stone.

As a fellow orphan, I felt Kyle's "pebble" was traveling a path that would take him to the treasure of the Stone as he matured, but instead he walked through a dark portal into a different mystery beyond time. The

Trickster had taken away the one most dear to me in this life. To begin my process of healing I felt the urge to appreciate the wholeness of my son, to balance the darkness of the mask, symbolic of death, with the golden brightness of the Chalice, symbolic of his life blood.

The Shining Chalice

During the two weeks following Kyle's death I stayed with his friends. We shared much sadness and tears and I was overwhelmed by the immense

The Shining Chalice is symbolic of the archetypal destiny given to Kyle and the fullness of life provided to him by its divine purpose.

respect and love they had for him. The expression of this affection filled more than four hours of a memorial service as many dozens of admirers stepped forward to honor him.

The details of the earlier and later years of Kyle's life in California were revealed to me by Kyle's closest friends. I was touched deeply by their revelations and gained a new appreciation of his life's work and his social life. As I record their stories I can see how they related to my earlier search for the Stone.

Memorial Testaments

Of the early years Mike wrote

"I first met Kyle when he moved into my town house at 204 Town Green Lane in Foster City, a young (18?), skinny, quiet kid. He didn't say much, since he was shy, plus I'm the type of person who takes a few weeks to open up to new acquaintances. After those few weeks, though, we started saying more to each other and becoming closer as friends.

Over time, especially as Kyle got a job in the game industry w/ Namco as a tester, we began to talk about work and other common interests and that's when I began to look at him more as a younger brother. His passion for games and his skill at design quickly moved him into the design role, and I always enjoyed talking with him about game development problems and hurdles. I liked to hear how he would tackle those problems—and I'd provide my input where I thought it would help. Kyle's eyes would always light up when he would talk about his accomplishments—that's how I knew he absolutely loved his job and was completely passionate about it. He was also very loyal to Namco, the company that gave him his start; even when I tried to help a recruiter hire him away, he didn't want to change companies—even for more money. It was never about the money with him, because he just enjoyed the work.

After Namco had a downsizing and laid Kyle off, in late 2002/early 2003, I felt terrible. I was working on a huge project at the time and we needed some additional design work, so naturally I thought of Kyle and we brought him on as a contractor. He knocked his responsibilities out of the park and to this day, I think about him whenever I play EVE Online,

162

because Kyle designed all the "named" modules in the game—nearly 3,500 of them—in only a month!

Shortly thereafter, Kyle landed a job with Crystal Dynamics, and I joined Eidos, the parent company of Crystal. Whenever we had monthly meetings at Crystal, I'd always make it a point to swing by his desk and mess around with him as a break from work. I could tell he enjoyed the company and job, because he always had a smile on his face when I saw him there."

About the later years in California, Harley provided me with insights into the more mature son and his genius.

"I've been convinced somewhere in my heart that there has been a terrible mistake and some other group of bereft people will be blindsided with all this sadness and pain and we'll have him back. Some part of me has known that this is all just a big misunderstanding; that Kyle will be amused and touched to learn that we have been mourning some other person in his stead when he comes back from the vacation we forgot he scheduled.

I had the excellent fortune to have Kyle as my right hand man for most of three years. I deeply respected and admired him and it has been hard going without him. The day I met Kyle was the day I started at a new company as a new head—a scary, scary day for anyone. My new boss walked me around a pit filled with a motley looking group of fellas and said, "this is your team." He introduced me around and I tried not to look either terrified or incomplete. I felt both.

Moments later, as I logged on to my computer for the first time and took a deep breath, Kyle walked into my cubicle. "What can I do for you boss? He asks. It was the first time of many times he would say that over the next three years, and it was the first truly friendly thing anyone said to me there.

That was Kyle. He sensed that I needed some help, and sensed that his quiet direction was all that existed of leadership amongst the guys, and his compassion and desire to have things be right for his team prompted him to do something that was very difficult for him; approach a stranger, strike up a conversation, establish a bond, hand over leadership to an unknown. Later, when we made his leadership official, he was a good lead for several reasons. He cared about his guys—professionally and personally, he wanted to see people get satisfaction and interest out of life.

But his quiet, inherent leadership wasn't even the reason we asked him to take on more responsibility. It was his genius as a developer that we wanted. These days, the word genius is thrown around pretty loosely. With Kyle, we need to turn to the old sense of the word to get the scope of his ability. Kyle had a genius of game design the way Einstein was a genius of physics, of DaVinci a genius of the Renaissance, In fact, I most often compare his ability to that of DaVinci. Kyle was the Renaissance man of gaming.

He could write dialog and storylines or engineer the mechanics of a large machine puzzle. He could establish the fundamental architecture of a room, find the right mythical back-story, or solve a difficult scripting problem. He could find the logic flaw in a game's story or predict a player's intuitive understanding of a puzzle. Kyle could design and tune systems as easily as he could knock out incredibly, interesting level layout.

His memory for the humanities was as phenomenal as his ability to sort through large amounts of data quickly. You could ask him the name of the offspring of such-and-such a mythical God / Goddess pairing, and he'd tell you the name in the original language and then give you the names of other gods who's myths were similar enough to be thought possibly the same story. Then he'd turn around and tell someone else all the places in the game that a slope less than 1 meter wide could be found. One of the things I always found amusing was that if he was not entirely sure of his answer, or was answering with an opinion, he'd always caveat it. Invariably, his unsure answers were right, and his opinions were based on facts and logic.

We learned to depend upon his abilities and took them for granted. Reviews of his work were based not on the idea that we'd able to improve on it, but on the idea that we needed to know what was going on in his sphere so that we could speak to it fluently. Losing him was a tremendous blow to the team—he was the center tent pole at the heart of the show, he was suddenly gone, and no one has the heart to find another one. Finally, we decided the only thing to do was to leave that space in memory to him—to continue on the way he thought he'd have wanted us to do. His team started turning to each other and asking, "What would Kyle do?"

But, oh, what we lost when we lost Kyle. Of all the incredible people I have met in this industry, his was the career I most wanted to see though to its end. He was of those talents who comes along so rarely as to be almost mystical in its right-place, right-time-ness. To have lost him so early is a blow to all of us—the games he would have designed at the apex of his career are lost with him, and that's a blow to all gamers everywhere

The only thing I remember clearly from last night's dream is sitting on the bank of a lake with Kyle. He was patiently trying to show me how to skip a rock—and those who know me know what a lost cause that would be. But he didn't give up, as long as I kept trying. Like always, he was willing to give as much time to my desire to learn something. All his friends and co-workers will remember the same thing about him. His talents and skills were never hoarded.

I can't imagine what it will be without him. Anyway, Kyle thanks for the visit. I'm glad to have known you and I hope you will stop by again soon, because I'll will be missing you something fierce for a long time and I can use all the help I can get with that."

A Letter to Kyle

As Kyle's father, I too felt the compulsion to write him a letter. I needed to express my respect for who he had become in life and my love for him. I reflected upon the parts of his life, his childhood in Texas and his later life

As your father I cherish the childhood memories you have given me. In addition I feel great pride for the man you became.

in California. During his memorial service those two lives became one. My letter to him is my way of integrating my loss with the recognition of his destiny, the brightness of his chalice.

Dear Kyle,

Son, I love you and miss your physical presence. At this lonely moment of depressing news and grief I am cherishing the memories gifted by your childhood experiences. First holding you, your first smile and words, your first crawling and walking, the firsts of everything happening during the early years of your growth that are so dear to a father's heart. Also I am appreciating the gift of the accompanying photos which facilitate the clarity of those memories.

Your shy timid nature, the willingness to please, made my parenting a light task, almost to the point of a fault. I chuckle each time I remember the phone call from your fifth grade teacher whose stern voice announced, "Don, I want you to know Kyle misbehaved in class today causing a disruption in our studies." Without hesitation I laughed and stated, "Good Lord, it is about time!" After a brief pause, she began laughing for she knew exactly what I meant.

The remembering also includes your childhood fear of people wearing masks. You even had a fear of Santa Claus. There are volumes of other details, fun stories filled with happiness and others of shared troubles, each relished for the feelings they have and are now giving. A sense of dearness mingles with my tears of sadness.

Throughout those early years you and I shared a fascination for mythological tales, the language of metaphor, bedtime stories from age nine to twelve years. We loved-ones took great pleasure in witnessing the manifestations of your music and art. Remember the fun of our explorations tromping into the Hill Country searching for artifacts and exciting visitations into the depths of large and small caves?

Later your fascination with computer games progressively took over your primary interest and became the inlet for your love of fantasy thinking. Your cats, Snuggles and Mister T, were contented to be nearby as you ventured into a playground of images challenging your capacity for intense focus and skilled hand-eye coordination.

Did you forgive me for sending you away at seventeen, after graduation from high school, for the dark "night of the soul" during the year that followed? Thanks to you, your subsequent accomplishments have unfettered any bonds of lingering regret for me. The young man you needed to become demanded containment in a creative lifestyle, a womb for rebirth as a young adult and an opportunity to become the individual you needed to be.

Life responded by the hand of a friend extended to you which compelled you to go in search of fulfillment in the "Golden State" of California. This twist of providence, an immortal dynamic, you subsequently thrived in the computer game industry which nurtured your creative soul where your unique aptitude for infusing computer images with the vitality of mythos flourished.

Son, do you have a laptop in the dimension where you now travel? Who needs one, right? You know your departure from this sentient reality has opened a file and a document that reveals the fullness of the myth you have lived. As your father I cherish your youth and now I feel great pride for the young adult you have become. Your chalice is now empty, but partaking of its contents you have magnificently fulfilled your destiny.

Although you are no longer physically present among us, the misty remains of your spirit haunts us and your stealthy presence continues to warm the heart of each person you "touch." We now understand what is meant by: "In the stillness is the dancing." A deeply feeling soul, comfortable with the inner world, you have listened for those insightful meanings which ignited your creativity and given value to your thoughts. From the evidence witnessed in your creative productions and the testimonials given by fellow workers that scenario of a highly creative life played out in a cacophony of productive and lucrative talents.

It warmed my heart to witness the testimonials announced during your memorial service? You have significantly enriched the lives of all those who knew and loved you.

Your interest in metaphor obviously opened you to those dimensions of mystery that actively influenced your fantasy of gamesmanship. I was amazed and delighted to discover that the subjects of your college studies; religion, mythology and philosophy indicated an early stage of deep exploration into your personal myth; the continuing quest for The Stone.

It gladdens your father's heart to know; during this journey you have come to know human love in a very deep sense, found fertile soil for your genius and fondly embraced its materialistic rewards. Your sense of worth was repeatedly validated in diverse dimensions. By traditional expectations, the duration of your life was brief. But your soul, in the game of life advanced through a portal and proceeded to the level of a greater mystery. You discovered an eternal unknowable meaning, "UNTOUCHED BY EONS" OF TIME.

The ruthless daemon of creativity had its way with you. Your creative introspective personality transformed myths into reality in your life and reflected in your gamesmanship. Because of my mythos experiences I fully appreciate how your ritual with the mask contributed to your living genius in ways otherwise logically inconceivable. Therefore I accept your fate with the true knowledge that it serviced an archetypal design.

Your physical absence leaves me with a deep, uneasy sense of adversity. I am compelled to perceive a portion of your connection to me by embracing the clarity of the Stone. You have an unending invitation to stroll in my misty mythos Garden, join me in my active imagination and visit my dreamtime at your leisure.

With my enduring love, Dad

The Dark Mask

Kyle's closest companion gave me an insightful clue, "For Kyle Grimalkin was not a name for a female grey cat but a male panther, sometimes gray, other times black. Kyle had a stealthy, mystical way about him. In addition he was very intelligent but kept mostly to himself, though not as much so in recent months."

With "feet of clay" I walked into an arena where dozens of deeply wounded souls gathered to lament the loss of Kyle. There was an overwhelming ambiance of sorrow permeating the stone walls of the building in which all present mourned the loss of a beloved companion. But even more striking was their glorification of him. I succumbed to the moment and allowed the demon of shameful exposure to have its way with me. Thus enchanted I was stuck with the idea that Kyle's death was due to some natural cause. This announcement had the intention of avoiding the unpleasant scenario surrounding the mask.

Upon entering Kyle's bedroom where he died, I immediately identified those dream images associated with the mask he wore during his last ritual. There were several versions of similar black masks placed about the room. That instant recognition of the blackness of the mask devastated me to the core of my soul. I spontaneously felt deep remorse and a sense of overwhelming darkness. I fled from the room loudly demanding. "Get them out of my sight!" The wisdom of Sophia lay hidden in the chaos of that emotionally charged moment and was unavailable to rationality.

I was caught up in the collective chaos of the initial emotional turmoil. Returning to The Way of the Stone I found my center and the necessity for objectivity. My candid revelation of the secret of Kyle's mask in writing this book aroused a reaction of emotional disfavor in a few of his loved ones. They sincerely believed Kyle was crying out, "Father why have you forsaken me?" In their minds I had done the "forbidden thing" by revealing his secret. I struggled with the intense censorship I felt from those loved ones who staunchly held to the belief that it was necessary to exclusively deify him. They felt the persona of his shining chalice must not be blemished at any cost which meant they insisted upon hiding his dark secret.

In private moments following the initial impact of my emotionally charged and directed responses I began my yoking process. Like Abraham I prepared to sacrifice my son's innocence upon an altar of mythos. According to the terminology of logos' thinking the cause of his death was asphyxiation that accidentally occurred during his final ritual with the mask. In addition, as a devotee to the Way of the Stone, it was my duty to reflect upon the mythological-archetypal nature of his life and death. This candescent process demands an attitude of candidness rather than an ego denial of the underlying purpose with some gratifying subterfuge. At the same time I honored the fact that all beings who reside in this world display an infinitely wide variety of perspectives generally known as levels of consciousness.

It is therefore an arduous task for me to "wrap words" around the darkness of the mask and to find reference points for those who love him and facilitate any understanding. Sophia, revealer of wisdom, announced that I must seek the mythos' meaning of the mask. My interface with the archetypal mystery of my son's life and his seemingly untimely death joyfully revealed his genius, which from my perspective included the contribution of understanding his most guarded personal secret, The Mask.

I must face my own maker with a truth untarnished. "There are no so-called secrets, good or bad, at the level of mystery now entertaining Kyle's presence." Candescent awareness comes to the Errant Orphan who is gone astray from the "right and good" values founded upon the rock. It is not the business of logos to point it out and make it a moral issue. Just as Eros can express itself inappropriately, so should his creative fantasy have become errant.

"Masks are instruments of possession. The mask transforms the dancer's body, he preserves his own individuality but uses the mask like some living or moving adjunct to incarnate another, spirit or mystical animal which is temporarily called into being and its powers tapped. But masks can bring their wearer into danger. When trying the vital force of another may in turn be "possessed' by the other."[1]

This unique portrayal of removing his mask reveals the presence of several animal creatures. It was as though he had removed his mask of innocence to reveal a hidden part of his identity. I viewed the product of his creativity with a sense of awe, but at the time I could not relate to the symbolism it presented.

During his life there had been an interesting interplay between himself and masks. Kyle possessed a childhood fear of masked people. It continued as an adult fascination with ritualistic masks and finally the mask became an instrument fulfilling his final destiny. He had admitted to a friend, "The mask is my greatest weakness." Rather than speculating for a logical answer concerning his drama, I now respectfully seek meaning via the foolish wisdom of mythos.

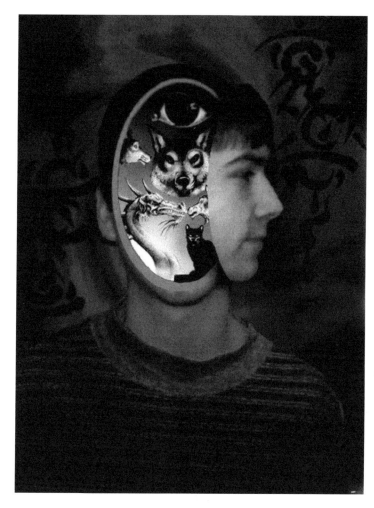

This computer generated picture was composed by Kyle at age sixteen years in a high school art class. It is one of many creations done by him during those teenage years.

The definition of genius from Roman mythology means, "Someone who talks to the gods." Harley's memorial presentation also described his "panther-like" personality and more, "With Kyle, we need to turn to the old sense of the word genius to get the scope of his ability. Kyle had a genius of game design the way Einstein was a genius of physics, of DaVinci a genius of the Renaissance. In fact, I most often compare his ability to that of DaVinci. Kyle was the Renaissance man of gaming."

I wondered whether Kyle was drawn to the mask to participate in dark erotic secrets or was it possible that unconsciously his use of the mask was a direct source of his genius. I pondered if genius arises like a bolt of candescence out of the darkness of chaos as a child of the shadow. Kyle's personality encompassed the vitality of anthropomorphic symbolism given by the Panther and lately the Jackal. He was an extraordinary being inhabited by a daemon and it is that which made him a hero.

The hero's journey was described by Jung. "On his way to his goal he conquers the parents and breaks his infantile ties. Once he has conquered this by gaining access to his symbolic equivalent, he can be born again. In this tie to the archetypal psyche lies the strength that gives the hero his extraordinary powers, his true genius."[1]

During each yearly visit Kyle shared some of his favorite videos. During the Christmas of 2006 we watched a complete season of the TV series, "Heroes," encompassing hours of shared viewing until 4 A.M. over two consecutive nights. The drama depicting the adventures of gifted young people fascinated and delighted me at the time. In retrospect I now appreciate and cherish the full extent of what he was sharing.

Redemption as freedom from grief confronted me with Kyle's brilliant chalice, and his secret was exemplified by the daemon behind his mask. I feel his genius was a natural by-product of yoking the chalice and mask and synchronously related to his early death. I reflected upon his life and how it corresponded to the Puer archetype he lived so fully.

The candescent Way of the Stone engaged me in a reflective experience of archetypal consciousness which has its own specific contents that emerge from unknown depths. They have become available to me for conscious illumination of my own personal interrelated drama through the conscious dance, the hymn, and the twelve disciplines. Devotion is my duty; redemption is the treasure. It is my pathway to the Divine Child.[2]

CHAPTER 12

REDEMPTION

Archetypes and Reflections

The mythos of the Stone, guided by Hermes and Sophia, expanded my orphan identity in the dimensions of the mystery which I found to be distinctly different from logos. Sophia is a quality of wisdom embodied in the mythos of archetypes. This uncommon thesis presents me with a problem. Jung's words: "being unable to communicate the things that are important to one self or for holding certain views which others find inadmissible." Nevertheless I wish to share my redemptive reflections with you.

The mythos awareness given to the reader by the contents of this book tells you that the dynamism the Stone is receptive to the meanings given by archetypal images. At this time of adversity I accept those images and the vitality they bring to the errant orphan who "wills to redeem." Therefore entering the sacred circle I remember Kyle by honoring the meaning of his life in those terms.

Although there are collective boundaries attempting to protect the individual from the dangers of psychic depths, they also deprive him or her of the individual experience of entering those depths. They thereby deny mythos, an exploration into the sacred mystery inherent in all of life. My errant way to redemption adds a unique archetypal level of reflection

175

and understanding for those interested folks who wish to embrace the total beauty and divine nature of my son's life and death preceding his passage into a mysterious idea called eternity.

"The dynamism of the Stone includes the mystery existing beyond those mental evaluations attached to concrete matter. For that mythic function the soul is receptive for archetypal images, underlying principle of all experience, and the vitality they bring to the diversity of mundane or sacred experiences."[1]

By dancing my visions with the twelve disciplines, archetypal images became messengers and suffering led insight. Consequently, self-pity, regret, anger, and guilt are in exodus from my soul. They are exiled to the towering top of Mount Olympus, home of the gods from whence they came.

Puer Aeternus

Kyle's chalice: "when Jesus referred to the cup, it is not simply his death to which he refers, but to the destiny which God offered him and he accepts his fate with true knowledge of its divine purpose."

A wide variety of Jungian authors have written about the diversity of the profiles for the archetypal Puer, but what follows are the reflections pertinent to Kyle and those of value to his father. This process begins by the insights gleaned from Marie von Franz's book, *The Problem of the Puer Aeternus*,[2]

"Puer Aeternus is the name of a god of antiquity. He is the god-child of eternal youth who remains too long in adolescent psychology."
He displays a youthful charm, charisma and is very interesting to talk to. He inspires the blossoming of things. He can work incessantly when fascinated or in a state of great enthusiasm.

He has a relatively close contact with the unconscious. He loves mythos. There is always a sense of mystery surrounding his quiet presence. He has a fondness for sly jokes and stealthy pranks. His creativity brings myths into reality. He loves the drama that transcends time.

His Achilles heel is his aversion for accepting responsibility. His youthful nature does not want to be burdened by any weight. He has a fascination with flight.

The main problem for the puer is not the lack of worldly reality, but lack of psychic reality (Stone). At some point, responsibilities of life demand a progression beyond this youthful stage of being."

Continuing, von Franz writes, "Nature has her own revenge. If a person cannot solve this problem (movement beyond adolescence), he generally gets punished with hellish diseases or accidents and it is not the business of others to point out and make it a moral issue.

Each individual has an inner growth to which one is attached; one cannot get away from it. This is what kills you, which means that if a person is completely infantile and has no other possibility, then not much will happen. The inner growth (progressive stages of life) in a person is a dangerous thing because you either say yes to it or you are killed by it. (The Mask.) There is no other choice. It is a destiny that has to be accepted.

This is how the shadow, in practical life, hits the Puer: he either crashes to his death in an airplane (accidental death or life ending disease), falls down the mountain which means to be thrown into the abyss. So you see this shadow has a double aspect: it contains the necessary vitality (Eros) and masculinity but, in addition to that, a possible destruction—something which might destroy the conscious part."

The Panther's Shadow Revealed

This is a picture depicting who Kyle was becoming during the last months of his life. It introduces an anthropomorphic mystery beyond my experience, a veiled secret for the uninitiated, but I do have certain insights provided by a reflective process, The Way of the Stone.

I am deeply impressed with the majestic pose and cunning facial expression of this Jackal personality holding his own mask. It is the portrait of a warrior knight with the full array of his armor. What a contrast to the personality of the Panther! I ask, "Does this shadow side of the Panther contain a double aspect?" As von Franz suggests: it contains the necessary vitality (Eros) and masculinity but, in addition to that, a possible destruction—something which might destroy the conscious part.

Kyle's primary personality, Puer Aeternus, did not survive the initiation from panther to jackal, thus he died "accidentally." The panther killed him rather than lose him to the jackal. This is the meaning given to me by the mythos of the Stone.

I AM ONE, BUT OPPOSED TO MYSELF

I reflected upon his life and it also reminded me of the archetypal "Puer Aeternus" he lived out so well; magna cum laude. That candescent realization led to my redemption from grief. It is through the mythos of the mask and its ritual that I recognized not only the purpose of Kyle's death, but the potential source of his genius as well as the instrument of his destiny. An "accident" was bound to happen. He also possessed two more common instruments for "accidental" death for the Puer—his Mercedes sport coupe and his racing motorcycle. They were parked in the driveway where he lived awaiting any other possibility of some "accidental" encounter with destiny.

Here are synonyms of accidental; occurring unexpectedly, unintentional, a chance happening. Synchronicity is also defined as a meaningful chance or an unexpected happening. There are things that come together in a meaningful way at the same moment, and when they do it may have a catastrophic outcome. It is a simultaneous yoking of an outer event with an inner archetypal mystery. I had to know what this could tell me about Kyle's "accidental" death!

You can see how von Franz's description of the puer fits my own perception of the archetypal pattern of my son's life and death, how the archetype demands its due, and how that awareness helps me integrate it into my own process. I have personally experienced the pattern of a synchronous life happening.

Whilst in the midst of my reflective process the "accidental" death of the actor Heath Ledger was in the news. It played heavily on my mind. It happened about one month after Kyle's so called "accidental" death. He was also near the same age, 28. At the moment of hearing the news I was hit with a candescent feeling of synchronicity. I saw a repeat pattern of the mask of destiny calling a child home.

Before his death Heath completed his complex role as the masked Joker in the movie *The Dark Knight*, with Oscar potential. It is a story about the mystery of masks which graphically portrays the potential for darkness existing within the matrix of all human souls and demonstrates the collective struggle with that dual paradigm of good and evil. The viewer certainly witnesses the destructive role of the Joker, Trickster, in a colossal demonstration of special effects.

Kyle's and Heath's lives and deaths fit the same basic archetypal pattern of the Puer Aeternus. It is also an amazing coincidence that Heath's movie, *The Dark Knight*, was released during July 08 while the game in which Kyle participated, *Tomb Raider: Underworld*, was released during December of the same year. This latest production is the eighth of the Tomb Raider Series.

According to a Crystal Dynamics release during Feb. 08, "One of the centerpieces in the *Tomb Raider: Underworld* will be the unraveling of the mystery surrounding the missing five days of the Mayan calendar, an apocalyptic time when the portal between the mortal realm and the underworld dissolve, allowing ill-intending deities to cause disaster and mayhem."

Lara Croft, heroine of the series, is a composite of Artemis, the feminine warrior, and the masculine Hermes, guide to the underworld. Both of these archetypal personality patterns are found in Greek mythology. Kyle was a major designer in producing this game. It appears to be almost prophetic of his mask of destiny. It is as if he played out his own destiny in the icons and strategies of the game.

My father, Kyle's grandfather, was also taken out of life at twenty-nine years of age by a rapidly advancing paralysis from multiple sclerosis which was his alternative to accidental death. As a consequence I was initiated into orphanhood for the next four years. As von Franz notes, history throughout time records the phenomenon of accidental or mysterious death of similarly creative young men at this stage of life. Each generation has benefited from the creativity manifested by this archetypal dynamism. Prominent examples from history are Alexander, Jesus, James Dean, and Ricky Nelson among countless others.

Among Kyle's diverse assortment of books I found a copy of my book, *Caduceus: A Physicians Quest for Healing*. There were book markers opening to the chapters, "Sacred Submission" and "Paradox Unmasked." The first chapter highlighted the chaos surrounding our move to Austin, Texas during 1987. The second contained the history of the woman who did not have the capacity to consciously integrate her alternate personality, the wolf, into her life. The third marker revealed the story of the mask, a patient with facial acne. The persona, mask, she wore at that time was not giving her a feeling of fulfillment. Her facial ugliness as a symbol of an inner process was telling her that it was a time for change. That mythos assumption was validated after she ritually sacrificed the attachments cherished by her current persona. After which she began a new life and her face regained its natural beauty.

Although Kyle never discussed any of those topics with me, I must assume that he personally related to them. He, like every human, had his favored persona given by the contents of his chalice and a "dark" companion represented by a mask. At sacred times his Eros compelled him to put on the costume to give it ritualistic and symbolic play. His dark companion provided a compensating ritual which made him feel more fully alive. At those times Eros related to him in his own way, surrounding him with captivating fantasy.

"Child at Heart"
Candice Pennington

Reunion

All the years of Kyle's life as a Puer gave me a sense of my own repressed creativity. His archetypal Puer features were eventually assumed by my inner dark brother, the Friar. With his physical death Kyle's essence now thrives in my heart, the realm of my creative imagination. My old man state revels in the essence of psychical reunion with his inner Puer. The birth of the Divine Child within this old man serves to yoke or reunite me with youthful creativity.

"Birth of the Divine Child is the Christ coming into consciousness. The ego reflected in the relationship of Christ to man. Sophia, to whom John refers on more than one occasion could easily be taken as the mother of the Divine Child."[3]

182

According to the archetypal dynamic, the yoking offers the potential for me to experience an expanded meaning complemented with a new enthusiasm for activities for my remaining life such as writing and storytelling. The memory of Kyle continues to invoke sadness mingled with feelings of joy. But … it is the mystery of archetypes and resolution of opposites that have healed my grieving heart.

By the act of regression, the loss of an outward flow of energy, the numinous effect of the archetypal Eros has been activated and has attained a different form of creative expression. The energy flowing back from this space activates its function in another way. The following reflections exemplify this phenomenon, the reunion of senex and puer.

There are prominent living examples demonstrating the difference between the senex and puer. Consider for a moment the personalities of U.S. presidents. Our forty-second president Bill Clinton is a charismatic Don Juan Puer; the forty-third is a Senex, either positive or negative depending on who is doing the projection; the most recently elected forty-fourth president is another charismatic Puer but of the messianic pattern. He is labeled either Christ or the Antichrist depending on who is doing the projection.

James Hillman in his book, *Puer Papers*, provides further valued insights into the archetypal dynamism which patterned Kyle's life and has influenced my Way of the Orphan's Stone.

"The single archetype merges into one: the Hero, the divine child, the figures of Eros, the psycho-pompos, Mercury and Hermes, the Trickster and the Messiah. The Puer figure brings myth into reality, presents himself in the reality of myth that transcends history." (All of those archetypal variations have participated in paving the Way of the Orphan Stone.)

Wise Old Fool

James Hillman continues and in the process I have gleaned a special wisdom from his writing and how it pertains to the maturation of my personal healing process.

"There has been an archetypal split between Puer and Senex (Latin for old man), beginning and end. As long as there is this split; it is difficult to say something good about one without saying something bad about the other. Paradox and symbol express the co-existence of polarity within the paradox. A two headed duality that is both logically absurd and symbolically true.

The negative Senex has lost his child. The archetypal core loses its inherent tension and is just dead in the midst of its brightness. Without the enthusiasm of the son, authority loses it idealism. It aspires to nothing other than its own perpetuation leading to tyranny and cynicism; for meaning cannot be sustained by structure and order alone.

Without folly it has no wisdom, only knowledge—serious and depressing, boarded in an academic vault or used for power. Negative Senex attitudes and behavior result from this split archetype, while positive attitudes and behavior reflect its unity, so the term positive Senex or wise old man refers merely to a transformed continuation of the Puer." I have come to fondly refer to the positive Senex as the "Wise Old Fool."[4]

My Puer-father and Puer-son were both taken out of life during their twenty-ninth year. I graduated from medical school at exactly the same age. I wondered what was responsible for the different outcomes. In psychological terms, I had early in life compensated for my irrational Puer dynamism by becoming possessed by the attributes of the opposite, and became a premature Senex, the directed thinker, seeker of rationality, advocate for informational knowledge, the "White Knight." As a result I lost my adolescence and as a teenager began a life as the classic "overachiever."

The suppression of my irrational poetic capacity for imagination was complete. I became a lonely wanderer who intellectually sought a home within the scientific community and favored the values of orthodoxy. During the interview for medical school I was asked about my grade of D for a poetry class found in my college transcript. My response was, "I discovered I was not a poet." The ideal antidote for the "toxicity" of my inferiority complex, the Puer, was accomplished by becoming a M.D. identified with logos of the rock—Major Deity in social terms.

I have now found a place to apply the previously unaccounted for sentence from Jung's Orphan Stone inscription,

"I AM YOUTH AND OLD MAN AT ONE AND THE SAME TIME."

I previously accepted the union of the Doctor with the Friar. I saw myself becoming an Elder. The logos bound definition of Elder implied an advanced age and defined me as "one who is superior in rank or influential member of a family or group," whose specific characterization is primarily dependent on the defining context. Not so for this old man! In retrospect I now see that my elder personality was the primary archetype that influenced the writing of my first book, *Caduceus: A Physician's Quest for Healing*. I even felt a little hidden pride when one of my friends called it, "A difficult read."

Since an Orphan of the Stone cannot be an elder on those terms it became apparent to me that there was another initiation in the offing; that of the wise old fool. The initiation provided by Kyle's death gave me a sense of the puer's archetypal variation. A reunion of my Elder and my mythosbound Puer (who had been freely lived out by Kyle) is now being offered to me by destiny. I have felt the creative presence of an archetypal Divine Child throughout sharing the Way of the Orphan Stone with you.[5]

It is transforming me into a fool. Gradually I am becoming an old man who has the freedom to openly laugh at mass conformity whenever the feeling of being astray strikes me. The forbidden things are lovingly embraced. Then without remorse, I joyfully suffer the consequences of that foolishness. This is the joyful state of being conscious of how to suffer from the perspective of mythos.

The high and mighty words of logos humbly bow before the mystery of mythos' underling archetypes: all human behavior and observed forms have become a conscious process of living the Way of The Stone. A unique stone, whose roughness amongst all those smooth rocks imparts the title of Wise Old Fool.

It is that solitary man or woman who enters a labyrinth seeking a redemptive avatar and finds instead an old fool who in wisdom expects you to take your own way to finding yourself. I find comfort in the justification of being such a solitary orphan stone where being alone is solitude rather than loneliness. For this orphan the Way of the Stone is redemptive. It transforms my suffering where slavery to some customary religious or secular doctrine has failed.

My life is enriched by such foolishness, and has become infinitely more interesting when I contrast the serious burden of authority carried by the Elder. The Way of the Stone naturally leads to the life of an old man whose foolishness is wise for a few stone seekers. I realize it is out of step with the logos bound mainstream but in step with the beat of my own drummer. I do not qualify as an elder, lawgiver, guru or prophet. I am not a master of the Stone but rather a humble facilitator of its Way; simply an old foolish heretic.

In the Middle Ages a great Sufi mystic, as he was being taken to be crucified, prayed, "O my Lord if you had taught these people what you have taught me, they would not be doing this to me. And if you had not taught me, this would not be happening to me."[6]

I began this book by quoting the wisdom Charles Shulz presented to me by way of his *Peanuts* cartoons. In the process of telling my story I have deepened my initial compassionate connection to Linus.

Lucy facing Linus says, "You are crazy, you are plain stupid, crazy! You talk like someone who's just fallen out of a tree. You are stark raving stupid!

Linus replies, "I should have known better. There are things I have learned never to discuss with people—religion, politics and the Great Pumpkin."

Linus' belief about the Great Pumpkin is symbolic of anyone with beliefs or practices not shared by the vast majority. It represents a metaphor for "The Way of the Orphan Stone." Maybe Linus represents the Divine Child after all.

Time will reveal the truth or folly of my assumptions as I integrate Kyle's gift of candescence, and his archetypal puer essence thrives on in my heart. My imagination massages its healing symbols and has become an infinite delight to my sense of being bathed in the light of mythos.

"The old man—divine child yoking means that each new inspiration requires a connection to soul bringing out the positive qualities of both. The psychic connection brings forth symbolic images arising from the archetypal view of things which can break through at the most simple level of reflection."[7]

With Kyle's death I felt the shock that broke the mold. I felt the heat that burned the heart of the elder. I felt the light of candescence that perhaps Merlin felt at his most foolish moments. The wisdom of the Stone is symbolic of the rejected jewel that accepted the Chalice as a cup of sweet bitterness. It is given to each of us and by which we both flourish and suffer and come to consciousness. The Holy Grail disappears into oblivion only to appear again when the twelve disciplines of yoking demanded a return to the quest for the Stone. The victim's trance state of bitterness or grief is broken by becoming "exempt from public haunt."

> Sweet are the uses of adversity,
> Which like the toad, ugly and venomous,
> Wears yet a precious jewel in his head;
> And this our life exempt from public haunt,
> Finds tongues in the trees, books in the running brooks,
> **Sermons in stones, and good in everything**
> — Shakespeare, "As you Like It," Act 2, sc.1, lines 12-17

The defining question put to me was as clear as the candescence of the sun, "Will I have the audacity to overtly suffer being a fool?" Am I willing to come out of the shadows and foolishly dance naked on Main Street during daylight rush hour. Perhaps this book is an auspicious beginning for what comes next! With Hermes' circle of stones serving as my Temenos, sacred space, the Way of the Orphan Stone to the wisdom of Sophia will show me.

Errant Cause

Solitude is my plight,
Dance shall be my action,
Mythos my insight,
And foolish my fashion,

Kindred souls of mythos
Remember and take stock
Within your own temenos
A Stone is a redeemed rock

Father and Son
Yoked together
Our destiny as one
Forever and forever, Amen

This 209-page manuscript was submitted for production on April Fools Day, 2009.

Acknowledgements

This picture of two celebrants taken a couple of decades ago signaled the initiation into a lasting and nurturing fellowship.

Jerry and Don

When the words of logos seem inadequate, it is the metaphor of poetry which comes to the rescue, so what could be more appropriate than one composed by Jerry.

Merlin and Hermes

Have Hermes and Merlin
Ever been known to have met
I do not know the answer
To this question, but, yet

When Hermes was known
As a man of the age,
Was Merlin a young buck
Or a wily old sage?

Did they walk about town
One shoe on and one off?
Were they naked or clad,
And did their friends scoff?

As they walked arm in arm
And discussed important things,
Cooked in a cauldron lots
Of dreams and wild schemes.

Hermes and Merlin
Were friends don't you see
They stomped town together
And spoke prophesy

They brewed up together
The philosopher's stone
And they learned all the secrets
Of the aspiring whale bone

Between the two of them,
Not much was missed
But a fare-the-well maiden
Who had never been kissed.
— Jerry Casebolt, January 2003

Our brotherhood has served the editing of this book whereby Jerry's expertise contributes to its structure and method of presentation. I, the author, and you, the reader, are both well served by his constant reminder, that the wisdom of composing is not only the telling, but also the showing.

I also wish to express my gratitude for the contributions made by Colleen Andrews. Her steadfast efforts made it possible to successfully navigate the way between writing and printing. And to all of you compassionate souls who not only loved Kyle but also shared your insights concerning his Chalice and Mask.

REFERENCE AND NOTES

Level One: Charting the Fray

Bollingen Stone

1. Jung, Carl, Memories, Dreams, Reflections, p. 356.
2. Ibid., 1, p. 227.

Adversity

Campbell, Joseph, *Power of Myth*, p. 3.

Level Two: Without a Kingdom

Errant Orphan

1. American Heritage Dictionary.
2. Edinger, Edward, *Ego and Archetype*, p. 267.
3. Jung, Carl, *Collected Works*, Vol. 13, par.2.
4. Campbell, Joseph, *Power of Myth*.
5. Jung, Carl, *Memories, Dreams, Reflections*, p. 452.
6. Edinger, Edward, *Ego and Archetype*, p.173.
7. Jung, Carl, *Memories, Dreams, Reflections*, p. 318.
8. Campbell, Joseph, *Power of Myth*, p. 151.

Wisdom of the Stone

1. Edinger, Edward, *Eternal Drama*, p. 27.
2. Ibid., 1.

3. Jung, Carl, *Collected Works*, Vol. 5, Para. 18.

Two kinds of thinking; Directed—logos; Fantasy-mythos

What happens when we do not think directly? Well, our thinking then lacks all leading ideas and sense of direction emanating from them. We no longer compel our thoughts along a definite track, but let them float, sink or rise according to their specific gravity. Thinking is sort of "inner acts of the will," and its absence necessarily leads to an "automatic play of ideas" (images). This type of thinking does not tire us; instead it leads away from reality into fantasies of the past and future. (Mythos) At this point thinking in verbal form ceases, images pile upon images, feeling upon feeling. In the process of interpreting a dream (physical illness), we abandon reflection and allow involuntary ideas (images) to emerge. It can be shown that all we ever get rid of are purposive ideas known to us; as soon as we have done this, unknown—or, as we inaccurately say, unconscious purposive ideas take charge and thereafter determine the course of the involuntary ideas.

The clearest expression of modern directed thinking is science and the techniques fostered by it. Both owe their existence simply and solely to energetic training in directed thinking. The great achievement of scholasticism was that it laid the foundations of a solidly built intellectual function, the sine qua non of modern science and technology. The culture-creating mind is ceaselessly employed in stripping of experience of everything subjective, and in devising formulas to harness the forces of nature and to express them in the best way possible. But, when directed thinking is no longer adaptive then psychic energy descends into the unconscious and there attaches to an unconscious focus. The process of fantasy thinking gives us the potential to listen to its message and release an unconscious creative impulse into a living experience

4. Carl Jung, *Collected Works*, Vol. 5, par. 224.

The manifestation of archetypes is not a question of inherited ideas, but of an inborn disposition to produce parallel thought formations or rather identical psychic structures common to all men, which I later called the archetypes of the collective unconscious. The archetype, as a glance at the history of religious phenomena will show, has a numinous effect

Arche: beginning, origin, primal source and principle. Position of a leader, supreme rule, a kind of dominate

Type: what is produced by a blow, imprint on a coin, pattern underlying form.

Archetype: The primal force and principle underlying pattern and form. "When there is only an image, it is simple a word-picture, like a corpuscle with no electric charge. It is of little consequence, just a word and nothing less. But if the image is charged with numinosity, that is, with psychic energy, then it becomes dynamic and will produce consequences."

"The unconscious, considered as the historical background of the human psyche, containing in concentrated form the entire succession of archetypes which from time immortal have determined the psychic structure as it now exists. They represent themselves in the form of mythological motifs and images, appearing often in identical form and always with a striking similarity in all races. Every item of psychic experience presents itself in an individual form, even though its deeper content is collective, archetypal; the eternal mythological dramas living themselves out repeatedly in our own personal lives."

5. Jung, Carl, *Collected Works*, Vol. 9-2, par. 282

6. Jung, Carl, *Collected Works*, Vol. 13, par. 277

7. Ibid., 6, par. 4.

8. Edinger, Edward, *The Eternal Drama*, p. 136

9. Hillman, James, *Suicide and the Soul*, p. 18

10. Hillman, James, *Facing the Gods*, p. 131

11. Jung, Carl, *Collected Works*, Vol. 5, par. 23

12. Campbell, Joseph, *Masks of God*, p. 505

13. Campbell, Joseph, *Transformation of Myth Through Time*, p. 251

Trickster

1. Barbara Babcock-Adams, "A Tolerated Margin of Mess": the Trickster and His Tales Reconsidered, Journal of the Folklore Institute, Vol. 11, no. 3, 1975: 147-186.

2. Jung, Carl, *Collected Works*, Vol.9-1, par. 456-88

3. Jung, Carl, *Collected Works*, Vol. 13, par. 24

4. Edinger, Edward, *Ego and Archetype*, p. 267

5. Jung, Carl, *Collected Works*, Vol. 5, par. 523

6. Campbell, Joseph, *Power of Myth*, p. 13

7. Jung, Carl, *Collected Works*, Vol. 6, par. 915-987

The Two Attitudes

It is impossible to carry out an evaluation that is independent of the influence of the dominant means of observation, subject's relationship to the object of experience. Awareness of the paradoxes in the uncertainty principle introduced by physics has added significance to the act of observation. In this regard Jung has differentiated two attitudes or mechanisms of adaptation. Both are present in the psyche of everyone, but typically only one aspect dominates.

Extraversion: The fate of this attitude is determined more by the objects of interest, the object acts like a magnet. An essential psychic content of the subject is projected into the object, to identify with its condition. Thus empathy is activated; the personality is motivated to acts of mercy and heroism, evangelistic zeal for a worthy cause, i.e., the crusaders.

Empathy is a movement of psychic energy towards the object in order to assimilate it and imbue it with emotional values. Although this attitude positively serves the weak and downtrodden "victim," it also robs the object of its spontaneous activity by making it a receptacle for subjective feelings. It provides no information about the random and unique. Therefore, the transformative value or purpose of individual experience is excluded.

Introversion: this state is an urge to abstraction rather than one of empathy. Interest does not move towards the object as it does in the extrovert, but is withdrawn into the subject. Instead one reflects upon the impressions an object makes upon him or herself, awareness that the object is revealing thoughts about one's own feelings.

His own world is a safe harbor, carefully tended and walled in garden, closed to the public and hidden from prying eyes. His own company is the best. He feels at home in his world, where changes can only be made by himself. His best work is done by his own resources, on his own initiative and in his own way. If ever he succeeds, after long wearisome struggles, in assimilating something alien to himself, he is capable of returning it to excellent account. His retreat onto himself is not a final renunciation of the world, but a search for quietude, where alone it is possible for him to make a contribution to the life of the community. This type of person is a victim of numerous misunderstandings—not unjustly—for he actually invites them. Nor can he be acquitted of the charge of taking secret delight in mystification.

Orientation is determined more by the inner self, the centre of interest where the subjective is paramount. There is the tendency to become submerged in this abstract reality, clinging to the guiding fiction derived from good and bad experiences of objects. As a consequence, exaggeration of this state of being tends to isolate one from life, thereby limits the possibilities that it presents, i.e., the hermit.

The personality of each human being possesses both functions, but one tends to dominate the nature of adaptive response to experience. Type differentiation begins very early in life, in some cases so early one must speak of it an innate.

The earliest sign of extraversion is the quick adaptation to the environment. Fear of objects is minimal, movement among them is quick and responsive, playing with objects freely and learning from them. Everything known is alluring.

One of the earliest signs of introversion in a child is a reflective, thoughtful manner, marked shyness, and even fear of unknown objects. Everything unknown is treated with mistrust. The child's real world is the inner one. "Still water runs deep."

Too further explore the human psyche's capability of response to the lifelong challenges the following summarizes the functions observed by Carl Jung,

The Four Functions

The conscious psyche is an apparatus for adaptation and orientation and consists of a number of different psychic functions. Among these we can distinguish four basic ones: sensation, thinking, feeling and intuition. Under sensation I include all perceptions by means of sensory organs; by thinking I mean the function of intellectual cognition and forming logical conclusions; feeling is a function of subjective evaluation; intuition I take as a perception by way of the unconscious or perhaps perception of unconscious contents.

There are many people who restrict themselves to the simple perception of concrete reality, without thinking about it or taking feeling values into account. I describe such people as sensation types. Others are exclusively oriented by what they think and simply cannot adapt to a situation which they are unable to understand intellectually. I call these people thinking types. Others, again, are guided in everything by feeling. They merely ask themselves whether a thing is pleasant or unpleasant and orient themselves by their feeling impressions. These are the feeling types. Finally, the intuitive concern themselves neither with ideas nor feeling reactions nor yet with the reality of things, but surrender themselves wholly to the lure of possibilities and abandon every situation in which no other possibilities can be scented.

In reality, however, these basic functions are seldom or never uniformly differentiated and equally at our disposal. As a rule one or other function occupies the foreground, while the rest remain undifferentiated in the background. (My doctor personality is feeling-sensation while my friar personality is feeling-intuition.)

While another it is determined more by his inner self, the centre of interest where the subject is the magnet. The personality of each human being possesses both functions, but one tends to dominate the nature of adaptation to experience.

8. Jung, Carl, Collected Works, Vol. 13, par. 476.

9. Jung, Carl, Collected Works, Vol. 14, par. 190.

10. Jung. Carl, Collected Works, Vol. 6, par. 374.

11. Jung, Carl, Collected Works, Vol. 8, par. 145-147.

The tendencies of the conscious and unconscious are the two factors that together make up the transcendent function. It is called the transcendent because it makes transition from one attitude to another organically possible, without loss of the unconscious. Constructive treatment of the unconscious is the question of meaning and purpose. Rather than questioning whether it is true or false?"

12. *American Heritage Dictionary.*

13. Jung, Carl, *Collected Works*, Vol. 8, par. 47.

14. Jung, Carl, *Collected Works*, Vol. 6, par. 310.

The Greek version of this myth has Pandora removing the lid of a great vessel releasing a swarm of sorrows allowing the earth to become full of evil. In the following text Spitteler's poetic version of this drama, utilized by Jung, is utilized to stir up archetypal images beyond the Greek version of her "unfortunate" deed, doing the forbidden thing, membership in the sorority of Eve and Psyche.

When Pandora delivers her gift to the world it means, psychologically, that an unconscious product of great value reaches the extraverted consciousness, i.e., it is seeking a relationship to the real world. Pandora's jewel symbolizes a regenerated attitude that has gestated in the unconscious. Its birth signifies a renewed possibility in life, a recovery of vitality. One has received Pandora's gift, been rescued from the wasteland, recovered the alchemical jewel of great value, discovered the Holy Grail or any one of numerous mythological motifs representative of archetypal Way of the Stone.

15. Suzuki, Shunryu, Zen Mind, Beginner's Mind, p. 21.

16. Jung, Carl, Collected Works, Vol. 10, par. 495

Level Three: Walking the Way

Yoking

1. Jung, Carl, Collected Works , Vol. 7, par. 78.

2. Eliade, Mircea, *Sacred and Profane*, p. 203.

3. Jung, Carl, *Memories, Dreams, Reflections*, p. 342.

4. Jung, Carl, *Collected Works*, Vol. 12, par. 126.

5. Hesse, Herman, *Siddhartha*, p. 11.

6. Corbin, Henry, *Alone with the Alone*, p. 189.

7. Ibid., 5, p. 117.

8. Jung, Carl, *Collected Works*. two implies opposition.

9. Jung, Carl, *Collected Works*, Vol. 11, par. 419.

10. Ibid., 6, p. 290.

11. Ibid., 6, p. 221-245.

"The heart is considered the organ that produces true knowledge, comprehensive intuition and gnosis by the mystics of all times and persuasions. It functions as an intermediary between the world of mystery and the sensible world. It produces symbolic images which are perceived by our imaginative function. In contrast the rational theologians prefer the use the idea of allegory.

It is the imagination which enables us to understand the meaning of suffering and death. By the means of those emerging image— ideas we perceive a deeper mystery beyond what is available to ego consciousness alone. The imagination separate from the subject has an autonomous reality on the plane of the intermediary world, the world of image ideas. It expresses knowledge otherwise inaccessible to the intellect.

The creativity of the heart is an essentially personal experience which cannot be regulated by the norms common to the collective. Every manifestation is correlative to the nature of consciousness to which it discloses itself. It signifies to see directly what cannot be seen by the senses or discipline of the rational intellect or collective faith. It is fundamental to the inner most being of the individual."

12. Chevaliar & Gheerbrant. *Dictionary of Symbols.*

13. Fourth Chakra= Mystical Heart.

7. Divine Love.
6. Psychic Energy.
5. Psychic images.

Above — Archetypal Awareness — Mystery

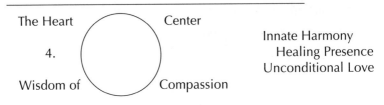

The Heart   Center

4.   Innate Harmony
                                            Healing Presence
                                            Unconditional Love

Wisdom of   Compassion

Below— Instinctual Functions-Survival

3. Emotions — Power
2. Sexual Libid. — Lust
1. Earthly Entanglement

Joseph Campbell adds:

"This is the sense of the second birth, when you begin to live out of the heart center. The lower three centers are not to be refuted but transcended, when they become subject to and servant to the heart."

14. Jung, Carl, *Collected Works*, Vol. 11, par. 415.

15. Jung, Carl, *Collected Works*, Vol. 13, par. 127.

16. Jung, Carl, *Collected Works*, Vol. 11, par. 741.

17. Jung, Carl, *Collected Works*, Vol. 11, par. 522.

18. Ibid., 6. par. 418.

19. Jung, Carl, *Collected Works*, Vol. 11, par. 427.

Christ's Hymn

1. Jung, Carl, *Collected Works*, Vol. 11, par. 415.

2. *American Heritage Dictionary.*

3. *American Heritage Dictionary.*

Twelve Disciplines

1. I will save and be saved.

1. Matthew 13: 46.

2. Doresse, Jean, *The Secret Books of Egyptian Gnostics*, 363, 366.

3. Jung, Carl, *Collected Works*, Vol. 8, par. 111.

4. Campbell, *Joseph, Power of Myth*, p. 123.

5. Jung, Carl, *Collected Works*, Vol. 14, par. 198.

6. John 14: 17 (Revised Standard Version).

7. Jung, Carl, *Collected Works*, Vol. 11, par. 434.

2. I will be freed and I will free.

1. *American Heritage Dictionary*.

2. Jung, Carl, *Collected Works*, Vol. 11, par. 390.

3. New Jerusalem Bible, Genesis — 45.

3. I will be wounded and I will wound.

1. Campbell, Joseph, *Power of Myth*, p. 160.

2. Jung, Carl, *Collected Works*, Vol. 13, par. 24.

4. I will be begotten and I will beget.

1. Jung, Carl, *Collected Works*, Vol. 18, par. 291.

5. I will eat and will be eaten.

1. Jung, Carl, *Collected Works*, Vol. 14, par. 523.

2. Jung, Carl, *Collected Works*, Vol. 9-2. Par. 126.

3. Jung, Carl, *Collected Works*, Vol. 11, par. 418.

4. Jung, Carl, *Collected Works*, Vol. 5, par. 224.

5. Jung, Carl, *Collected Works*, Vol. 6, par. 923–925.

Personal Secrets

(Something kept hidden from others only known to oneself.

"Whatever else maybe taking place in the obscure recesses of the psyche—and there is notorious many opinions about this—one thing is certain: it is the complexes (emotionally-toned contents having a certain amount of autonomy) which play the most important role here. The term "autonomous complex" has often met with opposition. The term is meant to indicate the capacity of complexes to resist conscious intentions and come and go as they please. Judging from all we know about them, they are psychic entities which are outside the control of the conscious mind. They have split off from consciousness and lead a separate existence in the dark realm of the unconscious, being at all times ready to hinder (conflict, emotional depression or anxiety and adaptive strife) or reinforce the conscious functioning (the seeds of the complex have fallen on fertile soil). It only means that something discordant, unassimilated and antagonistic, exists as an obstacle, but also as an incentive for greater effort (compensation) and so, perhaps, to new possibilities of achievement."

Transpersonal Mystery

(Essentially remains beyond full intellectual understanding or explanation.)

"The mysteries profaned and made public lose of their grace. "Cast not pearls before the swine." This attitude might have been a motive for silence. But the real reason was the imperative need to participate in a, or perhaps the secret without which life loses it supreme meaning. The secret is not really worth keeping, but the fact that it is obstinately kept reveals an equally persistent motive for keeping secrets and that is the real secret, the real mystery."

They denote an almost unendurable challenge, a psychic strait whose terrors only he knows who has passed through it. (Dark night of the soul) What one discovers about oneself and about man and the world is of such a nature that one would rather not speak of it; and besides, it is so difficult to put into words that one's courage fails at the very attempt."

The interpretation of its meaning, therefore, can start neither from the conscious alone nor from the unconscious alone, but only from their reciprocal relationship (the Round Dance). Inner images keep us from getting lost in personal retrospection. *Our feelings are imprisoned in memories*—unless we can reflect and translate them into images (metaphors).

The primordial image is the precursor of the idea and its matrix. It is not a datum of experience but is the underlying principle of all experience. It has one great advantage over the clarity of an idea and that is its vitality. It is a self-activating organism, "endowed with generative power." It represents the practical formula without which the apprehension of a new situation would be impossible. (As a mythic function) The image is an expression of the unconscious as well as the conscious situation of the moment.

The determining factor is primordial images. These images, ideas, beliefs, or ideals operate through a specific energy of the individual, which he cannot utilize at will, but is drawn out by images. There was a time when the utterances of mythology were entirely original, when they were numinous experiences and anyone who takes the trouble can observe those subjective experiences today."

6. Jung, Carl, *Collected Works*, Vol. 9-2, par. 426.

7. if an image is charged with numinosity—psychic energy.

6. I will be thought, being wholly spirit

1. Corbin, Henry, 1964, Mundus, Imaginalis
"My intention in proposing the two Latin words mundus imaginalis as a title was to circumscribe a precise mode of perception. The choice of the two words had begun to become inevitable for me some time ago, because I found impossible to content myself with the word imaginary for which I had to translate and describe. This by no means intended as a criticism of those whose language compels to have recourse with the word, since all of us are merely trying to revalue it in a positive sense.

The land of non-where to denote the absence of localization, its meaning is revealed in terms of lived experience. Crossing into this territory becomes meaningless at least in the terms of the meaning it has in the realm of sensible experience. It is not the movement from one locality to another, a bodily transfer from one place to another. It is leaving the where. Yet, having reached the interior, one finds oneself paradoxically on the outside of sensible experience. The equivalent of leaving the outer or natural appearances that cloak the hidden inner realities just as the almond is concealed in its shell.

Imagination is thus solidly placed around the axis of two other cognitive functions: its own world symbolizes with the worlds to which to which the other two functions correspond, sensible cognition and intellective cognition. I have proposed the Latin mundus imaginalis, because we must avoid any confusion between the object of imagination or imagining perception and what we call imaginary. The general tendency is to designate the imaginary as unreal; as it is customary to confuse symbol with allegory.

We thus have an intermediate world beyond the control of our sciences. It is only perceptible by imaginative function and the events can be lived only imaginative or imagining consciousness. And to find the courage to travel this road, we would have to ask ourselves what our reality is, the reality for us.

We are living in a scientific civilization, which has gained mastery over even images. Instead of the image being raised to the level of the world to which it belongs, instead of being invested with symbolic function that would lead to inner meaning, the image tends to be reduced simply to the level of sensible or intellectual perceptions and thus to be definitely degraded. The greater the success of this reduction, the more people lose their sense of the imaginal and the more they are condemned to producing fiction.

Although archetypal images, whose origin is irrational and irruption into this world is unforeseeable, their postulate cannot be rejected. The numinosity, ecstasy, which is inherent in them break through the mutual isolation of consciousness and its object, of thought and being. The movement out of our selves represents a change in our state of being."

In this imaginal reality the archetypal nature of human suffering, of knowing beauty and of the mystery of God, are known beyond the possibilities available from investigation of matter, intellectual cognition or idealistic allegories.

Those ideas have been derived through the discriminating thinking function during the last century. Jung intentionally, in his empirical calling, distanced his thinking from contamination by theological beliefs. All his concepts are very valid, but often controversial and difficult to comprehend by those minds conditioned with contemporary education.

Moving from the plane of those relatively recent learned thought processes, thinking about experiences of the psyche during the last century, we encounter a mysterious eternal world through mysticism. The feeling function comes into play. Its mode of operation is less discriminating and more intimately embraces experience by adding the intermediate realm, mundus imaginalis, between human consciousness and the indefinable divine mystery. Throughout the ages we have traditionally entertained ourselves with consciously derived secrets which tend to promote grandiosity or exclusivity."

2. Jung, Carl, *Collected Works*, Vol. 5, par. 223.

3. Jung, Carl, *Collected Works*, Vol. 6, par, 743–75.

4. Jung, Carl, *Collected Works*, Vol. 10, par. 38.

7. I will wash and I will be washed, Amen.

1. Jung, Carl, *Collected Works*, Vol. 8, par. 46.

What happens when we do not think directly? Well, our thinking then lacks all leading ideas and sense of direction emanating from them. We no longer compel our thoughts along a definite track, but let them float, sink or rise according to their specific gravity. Thinking is sort of "inner acts of the will," and its absence necessarily leads to an "automatic play of ideas" (images). This type of thinking does not tire us; instead it leads away from reality into fantasies of the past and future. (Mythos) At this point thinking in verbal form ceases, images pile upon images, feeling upon feeling. In the process of interpreting a dream (physical illness), we abandon reflection and allow involuntary ideas (images) to emerge. It can be shown that all we ever get rid of are purposive ideas known to us; as soon as we have done this, unknown—or, as we inaccurately say, unconscious purposive ideas take charge and thereafter determine the course of the involuntary ideas.

The clearest expression of modern directed thinking is science and the techniques fostered by it. Both owe their existence simply and solely to training in directed thinking. The great achievement of scholasticism was that it laid the foundations of a solidly built intellectual function, the sine qua non of modern science and technology.

2. Jung, Carl, *Collected Works*, Vol. 8, par. 2.

It is a generally recognized truth that physical events can be looked at in two ways: from the mechanistic and from the energetic standpoint. The mechanistic view is purely causal; it conceives an event as the effect of a cause, in the same sense that unchanging substances change their relations to another according to fixed laws. The energetic view on the other hand is in essence final; the event is traced back from effect to cause on the assumption that some kind of energy underlies the changes I phenomena. The symbolic interpretation of causes by means of the energetic standpoint is necessary for differentiation of the psyche, since unless facts are symbolically interpreted, the cause remain immutable substances which keep on operating.

The writings of the mystic hints must therefore depend on symbol and images in order to express their extraordinary experiences. The use of symbol does not serve the typical functions of ordained orthodoxy, but, instead, intimates something far more creative which has nothing to do with accumulation of occult knowledge or fulfillment of personal desire for power.

Unless you are an artist of some form or participating in Jungian analysis, activation of the imaginative portion of your cognitive function requires the use of stimulating techniques. There are many publications which provide them, but the one I favor is: "Inward Journey, Art as Therapy" by Margaret Frings Keyes and especially the chapter, "Awakening the Voice Within," p. 49

3. Jung, Carl, *Collected Works*, Vol. 8, par. 46:
Psychic development cannot be accomplished by intention and will alone; it needs the attraction of a symbol whose value quantum exceeds that of cause. But the formation of a symbol cannot take place until the mind has dealt long enough on the elemental facts. That is to say until the inner and outer necessities of the life process have brought about a transformation of energy. In civilized man the rationalism of consciousness, otherwise useful to him, proves to be a formidable obstacle to the frictionless transformation of energy. Reason always seeking to avoid what is unbearable antimony, taking on side, precludes any symbolic view of itself.

8. I will be united and I will unite

1. Jung, Carl, *Collected Works*, Vol. 8, par. 821.

9. A lamp am I to you that perceive me

1. Chevalier and Gheerbrant, *Dictionary of Symbols.*

2. Jung, Carl, *Collected Works*, Vol. 18, par. 521.

10. A mirror am I to you that know me

1. Arthur Schopenhauer, *The World as Will and Representation*, Vol. 1, p. 85.

2. Jung, Carl, *Collected Works*, Vol. 11, par. 428.

3. Chevalier and Gheerbrant, *Dictionary of Symbols.*

4. Ibid., 2. par. 427.

11. A door am I to you that knock on me.

1. Revelations 3: 20.

12. A way am I to you the wayfarer

1. von Franz, Marie Louise, *Essay: Methods of treatment in Analytical Psychology*, p. 88-99.

On Active Imagination

The four stages:

1. Empty one's mind from the trains of thought of the ego. This is already very difficult for some people who cannot stop what the Zen Buddhists call the "mad mind." It is easier to do it in painting and still easier to do it in sand play.

2. Let the unconscious phantasy image enter the field of inner attention. In contrast to Eastern techniques we welcome this image and do not dispel or ignore it. We focus upon it and here one has to look out two kinds of mistakes: either one focuses too much and thus arrests the image, fixing too literally so too speak. Or one focuses too little and then the images are apt to change too quickly—a kind of inner cinema begins to run. It is the intuitive who tend to fall into this trap.

3. Giving the phantasy some sort of expression; in writing it down, painting it, sculpting or noting the music one heard, or in dancing it. In the latter case the body comes into it that is sometimes very necessary, mainly when the emotions and inferior function are so unconscious that they are practically buried in the body. It also helps to perform a small ritual like lighting a candle or walking in a circle etc. because through it matter enters the play. Jung told me that this was more efficient than ordinary active imagination but he could not explain why. On this level two major mistakes can occur. One gives the phantasm too much aesthetical elaboration, it becomes a piece of art and in one's eagerness to cope with the form one overlooks the message or meaning of it. Or the other mistake is the reverse; one sketches the phantasm-content only in a sloppy way and jumps at once to asking after its meaning.

4. It is the ethical confrontation with whatever one has produced. The ego in active imagination must act like the everyday ego.

In the commentary by von Franz, she gives insights concerning the question about the involvement of the body in active imagination.

"Active imagination is actually very much concerned with the body but essentially with its basic chemical components in a symbolic meaning. I have often observed strong physical positive and negative reactions in the case of rightly or wrongly conducted active imagination. A great problem is raised by great affects and emotions.

205

Certain active imaginations can be done as conversations with inwardly perceived parts of one's body, or hearing them speak. Whenever matter is touched upon, be it inside or outside one's own body, there is a chance that markedly numerous synchronistic events will occur, which shows this form of active imagination is especially powerful. On the negative side it touches upon the subject of magic and its dangers.

A summary of other essential points:

Intuitive and thinking types as intellectuals take the third step of giving the phantasm a creative form as a mode of self expression which brings a great release, but is not "real" active imagination i.e., "Writing and Healing."

One important motif is the inner guide turns up. This can happen only when the therapist does not push the content as the guide, i.e., guided imagery. That is why one should not interfere with active imagination; not even a little bit!

Ritualistic forms of active imagination are especially powerful but also dangerous. It constellates a lot of synchronistic events, which can easily be misunderstood as magic. The borderline between active imagination and magic is sometimes very subtle. In magic there is always a desire or wish of the ego involved, either as a good intention or an evil destructive wish.

Finally, there is one more step about active imagination, namely, that one has to apply whatever is said, ordered or asked for in active imagination to ordinary life. Example; a man who promised his anima in active imagination to speak at least ten minutes with her every day in the immediate future. He then neglected it and fell into a very neurotic state before he realized that it was because he broke his promise."

2. Edinger, Edward, *Ego and Archetype*, p. 103.

3. Moore, Robert, The Archetype of Initiation, p. 38.

Mythos of Suffering

1. Jung, Carl, *Collected Works*, Vol. 11, par. 274.

2. *American Heritage Dictionary.*

3. Jung, Carl, *Collected Works*, Vol. 10, 160.

4. Jung, Carl, *Collected Works*, Vol. 11, par 417.

5. Jung, Carl. *Collected Works*, Vol. 11, par. 233.

6. Jung. Carl, *Collected Works*, Vol. 12, par. 152.

7. *San Francisco Examiner*, Oct. 1996;

"Chronic Illnesses Strain U.S. Health Care System," provides statistics concerning the growing population of Americans with chronic illnesses and the escalating economic consequences. The statistics showed that there were an estimated 100 million Americans suffering from chronic health problems with a projected 148 million by 2030."

Currently the most rapidly enlarging segment of the U. S. population is those people over 100 years of age. It is estimated that 50 per cent of the "baby boomers" will reach or exceed that age. So, the financial burden and the continued patient distress will benefit those in the "business" of chronic disease care, but not the one who suffers nor the society which must foot the escalating financial burden.

8. Jung, Carl, *Collected Works*, Vol. 8, par. 785-788.

9. Jung, Carl, *Collected Works*, Vol. 13, par. 1-84.

Level Four: To Sophia's Wisdom

Vision Quest

1. Jung, Carl, *Collected Works*, Vol. 13, par. 482.

2. Jung, Carl, *Collected Works*, Vol. 11, par. 418.

3. Chevalier and Gheerbrant, *Dictionary of Symbols*.

4. Campbell, Joseph, *Power of Myth*, p. 3.

5. Jung, Carl, *Collected Works*, Vol. 8, par. 2.

6. Summary: At this time of reflective thoughts and mystical critique: have the mythological encounters presented and ignited the imaginative faculty of my soul? Hopefully it is an activity stimulated by the use of metaphors whose meanings awaken those inner messengers as **images** which were previously unknown to me. Whereby, the unique spectrum of my personality was illuminated and enhanced through the power of my imagination, especially when facing the unpleasant challenges given to me by my life process. So, it is within mythological tales and psychological disciplines that I have discovered the Wisdom of Hermes, a spawning space for the propagation of healing incited by the presence of the Stone. That outcome was accomplished by the act of **communion**.

It is not my task to dictate "secrets" for anyone's general application, as explained in the Reception, but to illustrate a Way, but not The Way. For this orphan it consisted of applying my devotion to the twelve yoking disciplines:

The ritual of the vision quest activated the Round Dance which was engaged as a **solitary** feature characterized by **submission** to a transforming process. Fasting and free from the influence of cultural norms and interaction, I participated in the ritual by sacrificing my "total" dependency upon reductive thinking, logos, by contemplative **receptivity** for meaning which was provided by the **symbols** within mythos. My **wound** of uncertainty was given to the quest.

The focus on centering as **listening** with a beginner's mind gave me value to recognize images and give creditability to their symbolic messages. The creative response of Eros altered the title and contents of the manuscript. I discarded much of the specialized parts of the original, but **amplified** the meaning of others. By so doing the spotlight was focused on the Round Dance and its dynamic relationship to the Way of the Stone.

The **synchronistic** events happening around the appearance of the full moon further amplified my total experience. The dream like images enriched the character of nocturnal times supplemented by a **dream** that completed my full drama. The ongoing **reflection** appreciates the wealth of symbolism related to healing. It is an escape from the hunger of the logical mind for literal meanings and emphasized specific allegories.

Additionally meanings have been amplified thereby magnifying the interpretive possibilities while **active imagination** during the dialogue with the resident spirit completes the role call for each discipline's contribution to the total significance. The attributes of wholeness were fulfilled; the disciplines combined impact serving the function of yoking the mundane and transcendence, activated by the Round Dance ritual.

7. Edinger, Edward, *Ego and Archetype*, p. 102.

Chalice and Mask

1. Chevalier, Jean and Greerbrant, Alain, *Dictionary of Symbols*.

Redemption

1. Jung, Carl, *Collected Works*, Vol. 13, par. 124-132.

2. von Franz, Marie, *The Problem of the Puer Aeternus*.

3. Jung, Carl, *Collected Works*, Vol. 11, par. 713.

4. Hillman, James, *Puer Papers*.

5. Jung, Carl, *Collected Works*, Vol. 9-1, Par 259-305 .

Motif of the Divine Child

In psychological reality however, the empirical idea, "child" is only the means by which to express a psychic fact that cannot be formulated more exactly. Hence by the same token the mythological idea of a child is emphatically not a copy of the empirical child but a symbol clearly recognized as such; it is the wonder child, divine child, begotten, born and brought up in extraordinary circumstances, and not a human child.

The "child" paves the way for future change of the personality. It anticipates the figure that comes from synthesis of conscious and unconscious elements in the personality. It is a symbol that unites the opposites; a mediator, bringer of healing, that is, one who makes whole.

Abandonment, danger, etc. are all elaborations of the "child's" mysterious and miraculous birth. This statement describes a certain psychic experience of a creative nature; whose object is the emergence of a new and not yet known content which the conscious mind neither expects nor understands.

Child means something evolving toward independence. This it cannot do without detaching itself from its origins; abandonment is therefore a necessary condition, not just a concomitant symptom. As bringers of light, that is enlarging consciousness, they overcome darkness, which is to say they overcome a previous unconscious state. Higher consciousness, or knowledge going beyond our present day consciousness, is equivalent to being all alone in the world.

This conflict expresses the conflict between the bearer or symbol of higher consciousness and his surroundings. The conscious mind is caught in its conflict, and the combatant forces seem so overwhelming that the "child" as an isolated content bears no relationship to conscious factors. It is therefore is easily overlooked and falls back into the unconscious.

The "child" is born out of the womb of the unconscious, begotten out of the depths of human nature or living nature itself. (Sophia) It is the personification of the vital forces quite outside the range of our conscious mind; of ways and possibilities of which our one-sided conscious mind knows nothing. It represents the strongest, most ineluctable urge in every being, namely the urge to realize itself. The urge and compulsion to self realization is a law of nature and thus an invincible power. Its power revealed in the miraculous deeds of the child hero.

Progress and development are ideals not lightly rejected. The conscious mind, split off from its origins, incapable of realizing the meaning of the new state, then lapses all too easily into a situation far worse than the one from which the innovation was intended to free it. Meanwhile everything that has been overcome and left behind by "so called" progress sinks deeper into the unconscious, from which there re-emerges in the end a primitive condition of identity with the mass.

6. Campbell, Joseph, *Power of Myth*, p. 117.

7. Ibid., 4.